The Home Sommelier

Brigid O'Hora has spent over twenty years working in the wine industry. She began her training in Australia and since then has been a wine studies lecturer, held several posts as sommelier at prestigious restaurants in Paris, Boston, Sydney, Dublin and Clare and set up her own wine-tasting business, which she ran for three years.

Nowadays, between raising her triplet children on the beautiful island of Achill off the west coast of Ireland, Brigid works as a business development manager for Classic Drinks, an Irish wine company. And her passion remains spreading the joy of wine in a non-fussy, heartfelt manner, through food, joy and connection.

brideys_wine_chats

The Home Sommelier

Your down-to-earth guide to choosing good wine

Brigid O'Hora

HACHETTE
BOOKS
IRELAND

First published in Ireland in 2024 by
HACHETTE BOOKS IRELAND

1

A CIP catalogue record for this title is available from the British Library.

ISBN 9781399734615

Typeset in Neutraface Slab Text by
Palimpsest Book Production Limited, Falkirk, Stirlingshire

Printed and bound in Great Britain by
Clays Ltd, Elcograf S.p.A.

Hachette Books Ireland policy is to use papers that are natural, renewable
and recyclable products and made from wood grown in sustainable forests.
The logging and manufacturing processes are expected to conform
to the environmental regulations of the country of origin.

Hachette Books Ireland
8 Castlecourt Centre
Castleknock
Dublin 15, Ireland

A division of Hachette UK Ltd
Carmelite House, 50 Victoria Embankment, London EC4Y 0DZ

www.hachettebooksireland.ie

To William, Jude and Beatrice, my beautiful triplets. Everything I do is for you. I am so blessed by the endless love you show me. xxxx

Contents

Introduction

Starting Out on Your Wine Journey

According to Ernest Hemingway, 'Wine is the most sensual and the most intellectual of things.' Such wisdom, eh?

Personally, I prefer something more along the lines of Benjamin Franklin's, 'Wine makes daily living easier, less hurried, with fewer tensions and more tolerance' – now *that* fella seemed to be more on my wavelength about wine.

I don't know about you, but I get pretty exhausted by the nonsensical, wishy-washy vibes that can surround the wine world. All this talk of aromas of squished bananas and gun flint with flavours of bruised peaches and pencil lead can be a bit of a head-scratcher. I certainly have never aspired to have my wine taste like a rotten banana. Even discussions surrounding wine can be convoluted with empty words like 'structured', 'zesty' and 'vibrant' when describing a cheap Pinot Grigio or, indeed, a high-end, late-harvest German Riesling. There's still such an air of fanciful nothingness attached to wine.

Oceans of badly made wines are tarted up to sound like the most-savoured liquid that will ever pass your lips. The con continues. So if you have ever felt overwhelmed by wine terminology or lingo, don't worry. I have been there myself.

Choosing a wine off the shelf is like choosing a Smartie out of a packet: very often it's down to pot luck. There are all kinds of big wine brands - good, bad and truly excellent. Likewise, there are all sorts of smaller wine producers, also good, bad and incredibly special. So how do we choose what wine we want?

Wine buyers have many proven motivations, such as their knowledge of wine, food and travel, the influence of social media and their personal health. Other contributing factors may be wine awards, regions, grapes, the label (front and back), the weight of the bottle and its position on the shelf.

In this book, it is my aim to empower you to choose better wines and, in turn, enjoy the wine experience to a higher degree.

On a very basic level, I have a five-step method that I often use when I'm taking far too long in the wine section and I'm getting dagger looks from my children because they're bored, tired and want to go home. It's fairly foolproof, so before we get stuck into the world of wine, let's start off with this tried-and-tested method of mine.

Key questions to ask yourself when making a wine purchase:
1. What am I in the **mood** for (light and crisp or full-bodied and fruity)?
2. What food am I **eating**?

3. How much **money** do I want to spend?

4. What kind of **setting** will be I drinking my wine in?

5. **Who** will I be sharing my wine with?

Let's think of relevant examples to give each of these points some context.

What am I in the mood for?

As you roam through the daunting array of wines, first and foremost think to yourself about what mood you are in. Listen to your inner desires.

Are you energised after a gym session and feel like having a light, mouth-watering crisp Sauvignon Blanc or a Picpoul de Pinet? Perhaps it's a Friday evening and you're getting ready to hit the tiles, so you just want a light, low-alcohol wine like a crisp German Riesling to sip on while you get ready. Maybe you're completely wiped after a long, hard week, you're almost fit for a cry, and you're looking for a wine that will give you a veritable hug – a heart-warming Rioja Reserva red that demands an open fire and a hearty piece of cheese. Or perhaps it's a Sunday evening. You're looking to just have the one glass, and, in your mind, you know it's probably slightly healthier to stick to a glass of lighter-weight Beaujolais red. That way, if nothing else, you're getting some antioxidants into you.

It's a stretch to call it healthy, I know, but we all need tipping points to help us decide. So, for an occasion like this I'll take it.

What food am I eating?

There is many a wine sceptic who will argue the toss about whether or not a white should be paired with fish and a red with steak, blah, blah, blah. I will delve into food and wine pairings in much greater detail in Chapters 5 and 6, but, rest assured, if you're bringing home a fruit-driven white with plenty of oak, like an Australian Chardonnay, and you're pairing it with a lemon-drizzled ceviche, you will weep. The wine will totally overpower the delicately flavoured raw fish and all flavours will be lost. Furthermore, the excessive lemon on the fish will sour your buttery-style Chardonnay. Or maybe you have chosen a big, meaty Côtes du Rhône Villages and you're trying out that Dover sole you got fresh from the fish van. Forget it. It may as well be cardboard as you will not be tasting the delicacies of the fish.

Worse still, you have spent your hard-earned cash on a bottle of top-end Italian Gavi, a steely, crisp white wine that pierces through rich foods. But you're sipping it at a BBQ with gargantuan proportions of charred, smoky red meats, so disaster will strike. You may as well be firing your hard-earned cash straight on the BBQ and bypassing the wine altogether. There will be no pleasure from the watery attempt by Gavi. And that is not the wine producers' fault: it's the hot sauce's fault. It's a battle of wills, with no battle at all. The sauce will dominate the wine. And, yes, I've had many the eye roll in my own family home about the idealism of food and wine pairing and my bourgeois notions; however I, like many, do not want my precious wine spoiled by an over-bearing, lingering flavour.

How much money do I want to spend?

This would seem the most obvious of all points. As we know, wine can seem affordable and then suddenly creep up into astronomical prices that are enough to sting your eyes. My view on this is to try not to be too swayed with a certain number in your mind, as sale wines will always offer value.

What I mean by this is when you're planning to spend €12, having absolutely blitzed your card on clothes, concert tickets and a flight to Spain, you will naturally be adamant that your wine spending has to be restrained. And that's fair enough. Then out of nowhere your favourite wine, that normally retails at around €18, is reduced to €14! But, in your mind, you've already promised yourself you're not going over budget, and that's that. So, you go ahead and spend the €12 as promised on a bottle of wine you've never tasted before. You're proud of yourself for sticking to your guns – but when you arrive home, you taste the wine and it is completely not what you expected. It lacks a punch, it has a short finish and you're not so keen on the actual fruit flavours in the wine. And you think to yourself, for the sake of €2 you have decreased your enjoyment value by 90 per cent. For the sake of €2 you ended up not bothering with a second glass, it was that underwhelming.

On the other hand, if you had spent the extra €2, the value of your experience would have far exceeded your expectations.

This is one very important thing to note, because the value of the actual wine in the bottle is about €1, so if you spend the extra €2, the value and the quality of the juice increases by 200 per cent. So, by spending another €2 on your wine, you are effectively moving up into another quality level. The value of the wine in the bottle after transportation costs, productions costs and retail margins are removed from the price is minimal in comparison.

There are some exceptions to this 'rule' of spending more equalling increased value though, and it is generally large-branded wines that seem to have crept up in price drastically in the past number of years. If you are sticking to a smaller wine producer, generally the extra euro or two you spend will be reciprocated by the elevated juice in the bottle.

Here's the price breakdown:

Retail price	Packing and distribution	Tax (excise & VAT)	Remaining amount	% of VAT and excise
€9	€3.60	€4.87	€0.53	54%
€12	€4.80	€5.43	€1.77	45.3%
€18	€7.20	€6.56	€4.26	36.4%
€24	€9.60	€7.68	€6.72	32%

Source: Revenue Commissioners

Moral of the story, try not to have too-rigid a budget in your mind when you go to buy your wine - see what's on offer and take it from there.

Another point to make when considering the amount of money you want to spend is that when wines are on special offer, it is probably because the store needs to shift the existing stock to make way for the new vintage of that particular wine.

Unlike food, wine has a generous shelf life, so you don't need to worry about it going off the day after you've bought it. But the poor old producer is still making wine each year. So even though last year's vintage is still good to drink, the wine producer will still be looking to shift their most recent vintage.

Red wines are generally considered to have a slightly longer shelf life than white wines, and this is because of the extended skin contact that enhances tannins (natural compounds found in the skins, pips and stalks of grapes – they affect the textural feel of wine). Red wines are also known to have greater degrees of antioxidant properties than white wines. Antioxidants found in wine are called polyphenols and are known to protect your cells from damage. These nourishing antioxidants are found in the skins of the grapes. To make a red wine with plenty of colour, you leave the squished berry in contact with the skins for longer to leach extra colour and tannins. Whilst this extended time on the skins gives extra weight to the wine, it also leaches antioxidants in the juice of the wine.

As a complete generalisation, white wine in shops will last one to two years after the vintage on the bottle. Red wines will last three to four years. This is, of course, excluding higher end wines that have been produced to age for a very long time.

Because of the new legislation in Ireland on minimum alcohol pricing, a standard unit of alcohol can cost no less than €1. Each 750ml bottle of wine at 12% alcohol has 7.5 units of alcohol in it, therefore the cheapest bottle of wine should cost €7.50. However, some bottles of wine may be cheaper because they have a lower level of alcohol.

In Ireland, our lovely government adds a tax of €3.19 to every single bottle of wine that is sold and consumed here. So, the cheapest bottle of wine after tax, retail margins, transportation costs and production costs has a value of less than 50 cent for the actual juice in the bottle. As I mentioned earlier, if you are willing to add €2.50 to this, and pay €10, the value of the wine will increase to almost €2, and so on, and so on. By the time you're above the €20 price tag, the value of the wine has increased exponentially and the quality is miles ahead.

Wine is one of the few products in the world where spending an extra euro or two can make all the difference.

A general rule of thumb for wine pricing is dramatically different than what it was five years ago, and that's a sad fact. Thankfully, we have wine to cheer us up. My initial advice would be to spend a little more on your wine - enjoy it more and drink less. Quality is key. Having said that, consider €9 the new €7. For a wine of quality and character the sweet spot is €14-€18. Anything above this is a superior quality wine.

What kind of setting will be I drinking my wine in?

This is a really important question to ask yourself. Will you be drinking your wine in your kitchen or living room where it will be quiet and calm, and so you'll have the headspace to enjoy the wine? Are you bringing this bottle to a dinner party, where you may only enjoy half of a glass? Or, worse yet, are you heading to a house party, with loud music, lairy people and a heady mix of odours in a crowded room to add confusion to the mix? At a party, the sip-and-savour technique goes out the window, only to be replaced by the guzzling and chatting. The wine hasn't a hope of making an impression.

My point being, enjoying wine is a very sensory experience. Ideally, we take time to sip wine, think about the flavours and the feelings in our mouths. We reflect on the wine and conversation that can be had around the wine of the evening and all its intriguing attributes. So, if you have the time and the space to truly enjoy wine, this is when you spend a little extra on a bottle.

When you're bringing your bottle to a dinner party, yes, you still spend a little money on it, however, this time, you should be looking for more of a crowd-pleaser wine. Choose one of those well-known and well-loved wine regions, like Rioja made from the Tempranillo grape; Albariño from north-west Spain made from the Albariño grape; a Côtes du Rhône Villages made from soothing Grenache and Syrah; a Sancerre, the infamous French white, made from Sauvignon Blanc; a beefy Aussie Shiraz from Coonawarra; or a delicate steely white from northern Italy called Gavi di Gavi.

9

If you are heading to your friend of a friend's fortieth birthday party that's taking place in the house with DJs on each floor, plastic cups to drink from and no sign of a piece of cheese or indeed a cracker, that is when you head for the everyday big-brand wines. At a party like this, the host is more likely to recognise a big-brand wine and be grateful for your sentiment. Another reason to choose one of these wines is that it may be the only occasion where there are minus thoughts given to the fact the wine has no finish (or aftertaste) to it. Put it this way, the music is banging, you're chatting to a random stranger and the host is freaking in the background because the party has spun out of control. I can guarantee you, you and your new friend are not discussing the finer details of the wine or wondering how long the finish is. This is one of those times where much of the wine consumption is carried out in a subconscious manner. We are too busy to think about the wine because we are preoccupied with other frenetic things. Therefore, why would you bother spending good money on an expensive bottle of wine? Lord knows it could end up spilled over on the floor. Superior wine is lost on a gathering like this.

Who will I be sharing my wine with?

This point ties in with the previous one – know your audience. Be mindful of who you are sharing your wine with. If you're buying your wine to bring to your friend's house and they're one of those people who's happy to have a glass but doesn't think about it too much, this would be a time to bring a good-quality branded wine, like Cono Sur or Miguel Torres. They have recognisability and consistent quality. These wines are produced with novice wine drinkers in mind. Very often, they may have increased sugar levels that are used to appeal to a less-refined palate.

As your palate matures, you seek less and less sweetness in your foods and drinks. A seasoned wine drinker will seek wines that have those drying tannins, dusty notes of oak, earthy characters and extra layers of savoury tones to them. Those beginning their wine journey will often seek riper versions of these wines that will have a sweeter note to them because of the added or residual sugars.

Another example of choosing your wine carefully is knowing what sparkling wine to bring. You're heading to your best friend's hen party. She has booked a boat that will travel up and down the canal in the city. The atmosphere will be 'loosey goosey' and the craic will be ninety. Like at a house party, not one of her excitable guests will be examining the bubble content or comparing the flavours they're tasting. It will be less about swirling and sipping, and more about chugging and swigging – and that's fine. If you think about it, why would you spend €60 plus on a bottle of mass-branded Champagne when a bottle of Spumante Prosecco or a bottle of Cava is just as worthy a drink of choice? Furthermore, you have saved yourself a good €45!

An occasion where I would suggest taking your time and spending a little more when choosing your wine is when you get an invitation from the type of pal who has the potential to bore you to tears about the current on-trend chefs and avant-garde natural winemakers. Yawn, yawn, you think. This is the occasion where I would bring myself to my local independent wine shop and ask for their help. I can guarantee the beautiful wine nerds who work in these shops are just the loveliest people and are dying to chat to you in a non-stuffy way about the wines they stock. This is your guarantee that you will be armed with the right wine for the right occasion. Supermarkets are a very accessible way to purchase wine, but unfortunately, they often lack the trained staff who can guide you to the specific wine you are looking for. So, this can be a hit-and-miss scenario. There are supermarkets that spend time and money on social-media marketing, and this can help somewhat in educating you on their wines. So, if you're in the store check their social-media page and see if they help the endless and daunting trawl.

Now that we have looked at the motivators for choosing wine, let's roll up our sleeves and really get down to the nitty-gritty of how to choose wine that you will love. From learning about the most popular grape varieties to choosing the best wine pairings for everyday meals, my mission is to teach you how to taste and understand wine using straight-forward language. It is my aim to lead you through the world of wine, using everyday examples of foods we actually eat and wines we can actually access and afford.

There will be no talk of bruised peaches and crushed rocks,

but helpful descriptions, useful tips and handy tricks to enhance your everyday wine experience.

I began my wine-blogging journey on Instagram four years ago with a goal of 'no bull' involved, and I will stick to this exact same ethos in this wine guide for you.

My name is Brigid O'Hora, and I am a wine writer, wine lover, wine drinker and, most importantly, a wine communicator. I like to stick to the facts and keep to a low level of wine snobbery. I have spent over twenty years working in the industry – wine buying, wine writing, wine lecturing and as a sommelier. I have done all my studies up as far as the dreaded WEST level 4 Higher Diploma. This particularly scary exam has a fail rate of 75 per cent, so I am definitely glad that's done.

What I want is to spread the love and joy of this wholly sensual and incredible beverage. It is one of the oldest and most magical drinks to grace our planet. We must spread the good word and not intimidate those who gaze on from afar, too afraid to ask the wrong question. Wine should be an inclusive, not exclusive, binding liquid.

So, without further ado, let's begin.

Chapter 1

Sip Happens: The Ever-Evolving Life of Wine

> *Did you know?*
> *Toasting with a glass of wine started with actual toast.*
> *In ancient Rome, wine was known to be excessively*
> *acidic. Drinkers would add a piece of toasted bread*
> *into their cup to help cut through the acid.*

It was thirty-four degrees and baking hot. My fuzzball hair was looking fairly hideous. It was the mid 2000s and I hadn't got used to the shocking Sydney humidity since moving there from Ireland. And the notions of grandeur in the high-end restaurant where I was working were almost too much, but I ended up sticking it out for a year. I was a plastic backpacker, so to speak, arriving in Kings Cross straight after college with big dreams and a wheelie case. As I was teased by the staff about being a backpacker who might scavenge on the free food in the kitchen,

I kept my mind entertained by the prospect of making decent tips to travel up the Gold Coast later that year.

About 2pm on a particularly boring Tuesday, my waitressing shift was already sucking the life out of me. The scowling manager prowled the room to see what the productivity levels were. Mine were zilch, to be fair. I blame the heat. With a piercing glare from the prowling one, I reluctantly picked up the weighty, gigantic wine list. I had as much interest in this as I did in quantum mechanics.

The wine list resembled a copy of *Ulysses*.

It was viciously uninviting – long, complicated and a total bore to read. To inspire the gang working there, our head sommelier suggested some wine training. I jumped at the prospect like a cat on a hot Sydney roof. Anything to take my mind off my frizzy hair and the ratty manager.

The very first session involved a visit from the brand ambassador of LVMH – a French luxury-brand conglomerate that owns Louis Vuitton, Moët and Hennessy – bringing us through the full portfolio of Cloudy Bay. Of all wines to start my journey on, this one was a cracker. Needless to say, it is the all-out original – the 'OG' as the kids say – of New Zealand Sauvignon Blancs. Cloudy Bay was created by an Aussie man in the Marlborough region of New Zealand, and this style of wine was created to rival world-class Sauvignon Blancs, like Sancerre and Pouilly-Fumé. It became a globally iconic wine very quickly.

At that time, I didn't even know what a brand ambassador was, but this particular slick-and-sleek ambassador cleared the seas of confusion for us. By the time we had moved on to the Te Koko Chardonnay, we were putty in his hands.

To my surprise, I literally lapped up every word. Purely because he spoke like one of us, a normal person, and used words we could understand. There's nothing quite as irritating as a wine expert spewing empty, vague words that mean little to us mere mortals. It was the first time I had ever heard anyone speak about wine in layman's terms. And we, the gang of reprobate hipster waiters and too-cool-for-school bar staff, were here for it.

Up to that point, every time I walked into a shop and headed for the wine section, feelings of complete bafflement would take over. Rows and rows of wine on shelves is fairly over-whelming when you haven't a notion what you're looking for. Blind panic would normally set in if anyone came near me as I frantically scanned the shelves for a bottle. Most of the time, I would just go for whichever label caught my eye. And I'm a price-driven queen. Fanciful talk of 'bruised peaches' and 'white flowers' is not something I could relate to. I'm often a basic lass, gliding towards the old 'special offer' wines or the 'reduced to €12' wines! Boom, selection made.

Sauvignon Blanc was my tried and trusted best pal back in rainy Dublin. But asking me the difference between French Sauvignon and New Zealand Sauvignon was as good as asking me the difference between astrophysics and chemical physics. Not a notion nor single clue did I have.

Like so many others, I was a lost and wondering wine lover, too mortified to ask anyone in the shop for help. What if they realised that I knew absolutely nothing? Worse still, what if I asked the most hideous question, and then left myself wide open for copious ridicule and laughter all day long? It wouldn't be the first time, to be fair.

So, these newly planned wine-training sessions in work could not have come at a better time.

One of the first things I remember learning was how to tell if the wine was good or not. Best way to judge this is to check for the finish on the wine: is there one, or does the flavour die off straight away? One sign of a good-quality wine is one with a long finish, i.e. the taste lingers in the mouth. I still think, to this day, that this was one of the handiest tips I've ever learned. After a year of wine training each week, not only had I learned how to taste wine properly, I had also stopped the endless splurge of my hard-earned backpacker cash on bottles of absolute turpentine.

We were also reminded that one of the crucial factors in understanding wine was to understand how it was made and, ultimately, how it all began. How did humans create a vivacious and fun-loving juice from the humble grape? Truly it is a wild story, so let's delve in together.

Who, what, where, when and how of wine history

Over millennia, mankind has managed to transform a happy viticultural accident of producing alcohol-laden berries to a multi-billion-dollar global, precise art form and global industry. From the very primal beginnings of rotting fruit to caskets of wine that now cost millions of euros, it is hard to believe its evolution.

So, it is really important to take a quick look at how wine began before we continue to the rest of our wine journey. Not only will you shock the life out of your nearest and dearest with all your newfound trivia, but also it gives you some context for how the humble beginnings of primeval cavemen and -women led to seismic movements of global proportions in today's wine world.

100,000 BCE	8000 BCE	100 BCE	121 CE	1500s
Drunken monkeys	Georgia	Greeks	Romans	Monks

Drunken monkeys

In 2014, anthropologist Robert Dudley released a study called *The Drunken Monkey*. It hypothesised that early hominids (apes) in tropical forests were consuming rotting fruit 18 million years ago because these fruits were easy to smell and locate. This rotting fruit was literally fermenting on the trees. Furthermore, these sweet and bulging calorific berries were seen as a source of energy.

There is further evidence to support this as black-handed spider monkeys in Panama have been shown to seek out fermented fruit. Fermentation is the process whereby natural fruit sugars are turned into alcohol by crushing the berries and leaving them to rot. These squishy berries would have been alcohol-laden and filled with macrobiotics.

Dudley's study found that the mild effects of alcohol were said to ease the tensions in the jungle. The apes were always careful not to consume too much as this made them an easy target for predators. Dudley also suggested that at least 10 million years ago a critical gene mutation occurred in these primates that enabled the breakdown of alcohol to occur in the body up to forty times faster. Incredible stuff, really.

But how did it evolve into mankind taking the rotting berries and turning them into the thousands of styles of wines as we know them today?

Neolithics (10,000–2000 BCE)

There are many conflicting views, and certainly many a fable told, about how wine began. But the most factual version available today comes from an archaeological dig that took place in Georgia in 2015. Organic-grape compounds were found in clay jars in the southern part of the country, dating as far back as 6000 BCE. That's a staggering 8,000 years ago.

It is believed that these Neolithic stone-age farmers, primarily women, were foraging daily. Berries were a popular food source and grapes were stored in clay jars in the back of a cave and would be consumed at a later date. The natural gravity caused the skin of the berries to split from the weight of the grapes being crushed within the jar. When the yeast on the skin reacted with the natural sugars inside the grape, they had fermentation, which transformed these sugars into alcohol. Alongside alcohol, the other by-product is carbon dioxide.

**Natural sugars + yeast =
ethanol + carbon dioxide**

Naturally, no food item was ever wasted, so the crushed, mushy grapes were consumed. These Neolithic discoverers, unbeknownst to themselves, were the first to create a mean Merlot or a crisp Sauvignon Blanc. No doubt the effects of the alcohol were experienced on a psychotropic level. Furthermore, the natural carbon dioxide within the mush would have created a mouth-cleansing experience.

Effectively, this was the beginning of wine production in its most basic form. The simple process of storing berries that split within the jar sparked fermentation, leaving squishy alcohol-filled berries. Much like their primate brethren, you could say this period was the beginning of boozy lunches for mankind.

The ancient world (2500 BCE–374 CE)

Overtime, fermentation production was honed and toned to suit the style of wine desired. The massive trade throughout the world at the time led to the spread of wine production and vine growing.

There are Egyptian records of wine production dating as far back as 2500 BCE. The production was primarily for religious ceremonies, but it further highlights the widespread use of fermented fruits to create wine.

The Greeks and the Romans were incredibly important in the development of wine production. This was spurred on by their deep-rooted trading traditions. They would exchange olive oil, metalwork and pottery for grapevines, seeds and spices.

As time progressed, and their winemaking skills became more

apparent, they also discovered their own wealth of wild vines native to their lands. This began the evolution of vine growing and winemaking for the Mediterranean region, and soon after that the remainder of Europe.

In line with the opportunistic nature of the Ancient Greeks (1200-325 BCE), they began to understand their own vines suited their own climate. It was the Greeks who harnessed wine into their everyday lives, creating this notion of a modern wine culture.

Wine was used not only for religious services but also for symposiums. The literal Greek meaning for the word 'symposium' is 'to drink together'. These were events where Greeks would meet to drink, discuss and occasionally philosophise, usually held by aristocratic men for their peers, which became extremely popular. In our modern world, of course, this is the pub! Many of these rowdy, gregarious set-ups are often illustrated on old clay jars.

Further to this, wine was used for medicinal purposes, often proving healthier for people to consume than unsanitised water. Like so many aspects of Greek life, they had a god of wine, Dionysus, who was the god of winemaking, fertility, orchards, fruit, vegetation and insanity. He was also the god of religious ecstasy and festivity, and was considered the convivial god of life for all things joyful in Greek mythology. He was a busy man indeed.

The Romans (625 BCE-374 CE) took things one step further and made wine accessible for women, peasants, slaves and aristocrats alike. Like the Greeks, the Romans were convinced of its medicinal purposes, with writers advocating it for stomach issues, gout, animal bites and, funnily enough, memory loss.

It is believed that wine was so plentiful during the Roman Empire that it would flow down the streets during festivals and celebrations. By the end of the first century CE, Roman soldiers and civilians were said to be consuming a whopping 100 gallons a year. This equates to 1.04 litres per day! Many believe it was the Romans who first encouraged binge drinking, by playing drinking games at banquets.

What is interesting is the fact that Romans were celebrating the notion of vintages - reference to the year the wine was made. When the weather plays ball, and the fruit set is perfect with a generous warm harvest, the quality of the fruit is exceptional. By this time, the Romans were so far advanced in wine production that the climate, the site selection and the ageing process were all factors in improving the wine made each year. The vintage 121 CE was considered to be one of the finest of this era.

Coupled with chatter of vintages, the Romans were noted for the beginnings of barrel ageing. After transporting their wines in oak barrels for some time, they began to realise the beautiful oak flavours the barrels imparted - thus began the notion of ageing wines in new or old oak barrels. The Romans were enjoying flavours like toasted oak, coconut, leather and vanilla. All typical flavours we enjoy in today's modern wines.

Monks (1000–1500)

As the Romans conquered Europe, they brought their vines with them and planted them throughout western Europe in France, Spain, Portugal, Germany and Austria. But it was really the clergy who strengthened and perfected the wine industry within these countries. Most notably this was done by the Benedictine and Cistercian monks.

When you dig a little deeper into why wine regions like Burgundy (France), Bordeaux (France), the Mosel Valley (Germany), Priorat (Spain) and Rioja (Spain) are so successful and well established, you will find the monks are the troupe of hard-working, fastidious people behind it.

The most prominent religion around the Dark Ages was Catholicism. Initially, the Church's land was used to produce quality grapes for their own religious ceremonies. But, as time progressed and the success of selling expensive wines to the bourgeoisie of Europe became apparent, the monks truly honed their craft and began to focus on high-end production. Wines from Champagne, Burgundy and Bordeaux were at the forefront of the lavish banquets of the elite of Europe. The monks relished their generous profits and used their well-earned monies to develop wine regions even further.

New World wines (1700s)

In 1659, as the Dutch East India Company colonised South Africa, there was a demand for wine to supply the sailors. Vines were planted on suitable soils and wines were produced similar in style to the ones found in Europe. Similar Mediterranean climates and soil types lent a hand in igniting the beginnings of the wine industry in South Africa.

The first fleet, captained by Arthur Philip in 1787, on its way to Australia to establish the penal colony made a stop at the newly founded wine regions. Here they picked up vine cuttings, grapes and production techniques to bring with them to Australia and New Zealand where vines were planted to supply the British conquistadors.

What was interesting about this particular influx of vines and vine culture was that this was the only 'dry' continent at the time. The Indigenous Aboriginal peoples were one of the few societies in the world that had no tradition linked to fermenting fruits for alcoholic beverages. By the late 1700s, the rest of the globe had adapted their cultures to fermenting and consuming alcohol. This mitigating factor was believed to be one of the primary reasons for slowing the development of the wine industry in Australia.

One important figure in winemaking and development in Australia and New Zealand was a British man named James Busby. He is considered to be the father of the wine industry there, promoting winemaking and integration of wine culture throughout first Australia and then New Zealand in 1836.

By the 1890s, wine regions such as Hunter Valley and Barossa had been established. There was a concentration on sweeter, fortified wines for an extended time. However, by the early 1980s, a rise in innovation and development saw a major shift towards large-scale production of drier wines that had a major marketability to them. Their popularity in the Irish and

English domestic markets began to rise rapidly. They were creating sun-filled, fruity wines that were cleverly and colourfully labelled and appealing to the eye.

In South America, much of the wine influx came from the settlement of the French and Spanish winemakers who had lost a massive amount of their vines to the vine disease that was rampant through European vineyards in the late 1800s.

They were primarily located in Chile and Argentina, because of favourable soils and the beautiful dry, sunny climate found in the foothills of the Andes Mountains. To this day, some of the most prestigious and celebrious wineries are still producing stellar-quality wines in Chile and Argentina, including Torres, Mouton Rothschild and Opus One.

World's best wines

Naturally, the history of wine is far more nuanced and detailed but for the purpose of context it is important to have a general overview of how it all began, who developed it and how.

Of course, it is wonderful to have a look at the history of wine to get a real sense of the hows and the whys, but the purpose of this book is to teach you how to taste wine properly and show you where the best wine-producing regions are right now.

On the following pages is a list of the top ten winemaking countries and the top ten wine regions with a brief overview of their wines and grapes.

> *Top Tip*
> *When you are trying to decide what style of*
> *wine you would like, generally the warmer*
> *the climate the vines are grown in, the riper*
> *the berries will be, so the flavours will be*
> *sweeter and the alcohol will be higher.*

Top ten winemaking countries

1. France (45.6 million litres per year)

It is impossible to have a wine conversation without mentioning France. It is at the beating heart of the wine world. Many think that wine was invented here but, as we now know, it was invented in Georgia. Truthfully, most of the French success lies with blessed soils, favourable climates and the history of the clergy and their important role in the development of wine. The Benedictine and Cistercian monks are responsible for the likes of Burgundy and Bordeaux, which are some of the world's most expensive and well-made wines. Wine has also been integrated on a healthy scale into their Mediterranean diet. The French are famed for having a small glass with their lunch and dinner every day, reaping the rewards of all those healthy antioxidants without the overload of toxicity from the alcohol. Balance is key here.

2. Italy (49.8 million litres per year)

Italy produces 19 per cent of the world's wine from some of their incredible wine regions. Like the French, wine is part of their daily gastronomic culture and a little tumbler of wine is enjoyed with food in whichever region you are in. Wine is produced all over the country, from the northern Alps to the volcanos of the south. They also enjoy a stunning Mediterranean climate all over the peninsula, with the benefit of incredible soils, the Apennine Mountains, which create endless micro-climates, and a long and established wine culture that dates back to the fastidious Romans. There was a small group of dynamic wine producers who grew tired of the archaic wine laws here in the 1980s. They broke all the rules and started making wines using imported French grapes like Merlot and Cabernet Sauvignon. The irony is the grapes really thrived and so the quality and reputation of these demoted winemakers began to excel. These maverick, rule-bending producers now create wines that are nick-named 'Super Tuscans' and can fetch serious prices, €800 plus a bottle. David Beckham is famously a big fan of these wines.

3. Spain (37.6 million litres per year)

The Iberian Peninsula has the largest vineyard surface area in the world, with over 100 qualified wine-quality regions. Throughout Spain, all types of wine are created – from light, crisp white wines in Rueda to high-quality sparkling wines called Cava in Penedès to rich, robust dark-black wines in

Priorat. This land is blessed with indigenous vines that thrive in the array of climatic conditions that occur in Spain. This fortunate country boasts some of the finest fortified wines in the world – sherry – in Jerez. The Spaniards take complete pride in their unique wines and have some of the strictest wine laws in the world.

4. Australia (12.7 million litres per year)

Australia has had great success with selling its wines in Ireland. It would be unfair to pigeonhole Australia as the land of branded wines because it is filled with quality-driven smaller producers. Although they battle with the heat, and their wineries are facing challenges of smoke taint (due to wildfires), these winemakers are incredibly dynamic and resilient. Having spent over a year in Australia working in a high-end restaurant with the most exquisite wine list, I have had the opportunity to taste some incredibly well-made wines. Look out for wines made in Margaret River (Western Australia), Tasmania, Barossa Valley (South Australia) and Hunter Valley (New South Wales). There is a wide array of quality wines made from mostly French grapes, such as Merlot, Sauvignon Blanc, Chardonnay and, most importantly, Syrah, which is known locally as Shiraz.

5. Chile (12.4 million litres per year)

Far too many people have a bad opinion of Chilean wines, when they are, in fact, some of the best-quality wines for the price on the market. There is a big influence from the French and Spanish from when they settled here in the late 1800s from their own devastated wine regions. They have a strong and well-established wine culture and, most importantly, a strong work ethic. The Pacific Ocean combined with the Andes Mountains and the Atacama Desert mean these soils are completely free from the crippling vine louse, Phylloxera. Chile has the healthiest soils in the world for vine growing. With a similar climate and culture to Europe, it is clear to see why the wine world looks to Chile for high-quality, high-value wines.

6. Argentina (11.5 million litres per year)

Similar to Chile, the French and Spanish settlers to Argentina brought their own vine cuttings and viticultural prowess. The Andes Mountains straddle Chile and Argentina, which creates a constant supply of fresh water from the melting snow, but also endless microclimates to suit the particular grape being grown. Long sunshine hours and cold nights leave the grapes hanging for longer on the vine, thus creating more interesting flavours from the extended exposure to increased mineral and nutrient content from the healthy soils. Mendoza is a globally famous region now for producing serious-quality Malbec. Malbec is originally a grape from Bordeaux, but since its introduction to Argentinian soils and climate, winemakers there have managed to create a cult global style of red.

7. Germany (8.9 million litres per year)

I would be remiss to create a top ten list of wine-producing countries without including one of the oldest and most culturally infused areas. So many people consider German wines to be sweet and godawful, but this could not be further from the truth. Most wine nerds like myself will proclaim their undying love for German Riesling – which are some of the longest-aged wines in the world. In the list of most expensive wines in the world, you will often see a Mosel Riesling. And this is often because it is so old and still in incredible condition. Apart from Riesling, Pinot Noir also fares very well here – it is silky, fruity and so easy to drink. The best part is these wines have generally lower alcohol levels because of the lower number of sunshine hours. I urge you to venture out and buy yourself a dry German Riesling and try it with prawns or cured meats. You will be thanking me. Look out for wines from the Mosel Valley, Rheingau and Baden.

8. South Africa (10.1 million litres per year)

South Africa is one of the forgotten wine countries for Irish consumers. I've often chatted with my wine peers on why this is. There are a number of factors at play. One of the most important is the lack of a South African wine board in Ireland. But also there are copious political and societal barriers that have occurred over the years for the exportation of these wines into Ireland. However, the wines themselves are, for the most part, great quality. Like Chile and Argentina, there has been a strong influence from Europe on its history of vine planting and winemaking. Mediterranean climates dominate the coastal vineyards, and inland long sunny days and cool nights enable longer ripening seasons, excellent for vine growing. Look out for wines from Stellenbosch, Paarl, Cape Town and Franshoek.

9. USA (22.4 million litres per year)

The majority of wine made in America is on the west coast. A staggering 90 per cent is produced in California, with Oregon coming in at about 5 per cent. There are other wine regions, like Finger Lakes in New York state, and some bulk wines made in Texas. Similar to other New World countries, the predominance of winemaking occurs in areas that have typically Mediterranean climates, with mild winters and warm summers.

One of the most quality-driven regions is Napa Valley in California, which was heavily invested in by the French, specifically Bordeaux and Champagne producers. The soils are favourable, the climate is suitable and the pockets are big because of its location beside Silicon Valley, a playground for the wealthier winemaker. So American winemakers tend to concentrate on French grapes, like Chardonnay and Pinot Noir. In recent times, there has been a big movement towards using Rhône Valley grapes, and even a small group of maverick producers calling themselves the 'Rhône Rangers'. The tumultuous years of prohibition had slightly scuppered the immersive integration of a wine culture in America, however this seems to be changing. Wines from Napa and Oregon are expensive, but the quality is there. Again, like many of the other New World countries, brands tend to dominate. Ernest & Julio Gallo was started by two brothers in the 1930s and is now said to be worth $9.5 billion, making them one of the wealthiest families in America. Look out for wines from Sonoma, Russian River and Oregon.

10. Portugal (6.8 million litres per year)

For such a tiny country, the level of wine production is incredible. Much like its European neighbours, Portugal is steeped in vine history and the Portuguese have long been producing wines to match their local cuisine. From the very top of the country at the Spanish border to the Algarve in the south, each region has its own unique grape and unique style of wine. Vinho Verde is the fresh and zesty low-alcohol white wine that is tailor-made with fried fish in mind. Alentejo reds from the south are warm, fruity and robust enough for those barbecued meats. And, of course, we can't forget about one of the most famous wines in the world – port, the jewel of the Douro Valley. This is a fortified wine that has been celebrated for centuries. The English have had a long affinity with port. And this is evident with some of the top house names: Osborne, Taylor's, Churchill's and Cockburn's. Look out for wines from Douro Valley, Alentejo, Vinho Verde and Dao.

Top ten wine regions

1. Bordeaux, France

There are over 9,000 wineries in this geographically small region; 88 per cent of the wines here are red.

Wines: Médoc, Graves, Saint-Émilion, Margaux, Sauternes, Pomerol

Main grapes: Merlot, Cabernet Sauvignon, Sauvignon Blanc

Wine styles: Rich, full-bodied tannic red wines; crisp, fragrant white wines.

Price range: From basic everyday wine (€12–15) to extremely expensive high-end wines that are sold through auction houses.

2. Burgundy, France

The region is dominated by tiny plots that produce very long-ageing and serious wines.

Wines: Chablis, Puligny-Montrachet, Meursault, Nuits-Saint-Georges, Mâcon-Villages

Main grapes: Pinot Noir, Chardonnay

Wine styles: Paler red wines that are rich, silky and aromatic; white wines are often delicately oaked and give extra flavours of butter and pastry to fruity notes.

Price range: Start at medium range (€20–30) and go up to astronomical prices that can reflect the price of a car for one bottle.

3. Loire Valley, France

This region is the homestead to Sauvignon Blanc and produces the world's finest versions.

Wines: Sancerre, Pouilly-Fumé, Touraine, Vouvray, Chinon

Main grapes: Sauvignon Blanc, Chenin Blanc, Cabernet Franc

Wine styles: Home of the original grassy, green-apple Sauvignon Blanc that is popular the world over; red wines are light and silky with earthy tones.

Price range: Wines start from everyday quality to a small number of wines that reach mid to high range.

4. Champagne, France

This region is synonymous with high-end sparkling wines. It is now illegal to use the term 'Champagne' for any sparkling wine that isn't produced here.

Wines: Champagne, Blanc de Blanc Champagne, Blanc de Noirs Champagne, Vintage Champagne

Main grapes: Chardonnay, Pinot Noir, Pinot Meunier

Wine styles: Sparkling white and rosé wines.

Price range: These wines start from a mid-price range right up to eye-watering prices for a bottle of Vintage Champagne.

5. Veneto, Italy

This region, which surrounds the stunning city of Venice, is the powerhouse of Italian wines, producing far more than its closest counterparts, Sicily and Puglia, combined.

Main grapes: Glera, Pinot Grigio, Garganega, Corvina, Molinara and Rondinella

Wines: Soave, Prosecco, Pinot Grigio, Valpolicella, Amarone

Wine styles: Sparkling Prosecco, light and crisp Pinot Grigio, aromatic Soave and soft and supple Valpolicella. Veneto is also the home of the infamous rich and highly expressive Amarone wine, which is considered to be one of the great Italian reds.

Price range: From drastically cheap (€8-9) to drastically expensive, and everything in between.

6. Rioja, Spain

This region is over a thousand years old and is heavily influenced by the Bordelaise (Bordeaux wine producers) that settled here in the late 1800s. They brought small oak barrels and, to this day, they style their reds on the length of time they have oaked their wines. If you stopped producing Rioja reds tomorrow, the region would have enough wine to last for the next five years from underground cellars in the region.

Wines: Rioja Joven, Crianza, Reserva, Gran Reserva, Rioja Blanco

Main grapes: Tempranillo, Garnacha, Viura (Macabeo)

Wine styles: Oak-aged reds dominate; a small percentage of the production goes to fruit-driven, nutty white wines.

Price range: Some of the best value-for-money wines in Europe. Prices can range from cheap to very expensive.

7. Languedoc Roussillon, France

This region starts at Perpignan near the Spanish border and stretches the whole way over to Nice and up to Toulouse. It is one of the single largest and quality-driven wine regions in the world.

Wines: Minervois, Corbières, Saint-Chinian, Picpoul de Pinet, Limoux

Main grapes: Syrah, Grenache, Mourvèdre, Picpoul, Chardonnay

Wine styles: There is a rich tapestry of styles of wines found here. Value-driven red wines that are soft, juicy, fruit-driven and meaty; white wines that are generally packed with fruit flavours and have a zingy freshness to them. It also produces fine sweet wines and some sparkling wines.

Price range: From bargain-basement wines to value-driven, medium-priced wines.

8. Tuscany, Italy

One of the main wine regions here is Chianti. It is one of the oldest wine regions in Italy and is famed for providing quality reds that uniquely pair so well with tomato-based sauces.

Wines: Chianti, Chianti Classico, Verdicchio dei Castelli di Jesi, Vin Santo

Main grapes: Sangiovese, Cabernet Sauvignon, Merlot, Verdicchio

Wine styles: Medium-weight reds that have bright-red fruits and a cleansing finish; aromatic whites that have unique flavours of baked lemons and dried straw; dark, nutty sweet wines.

Price range: From super cheap to outlandishly expensive.

9. Rhône Valley, France

The Rhône Valley was long considered the workhorse region of France with the dizzying array of cooperatives producing bland and non-descript Côtes du Rhône in the 1980s. But through the guile of prolific producers with major vision and dynamism, the region has been elevated again to global superstar heights. Châteauneuf-du-Pape steals the show on a world scale.

Wines: Côtes du Rhône, Gigondas, Vacqueyras, Saint-Joseph, Condrieu, Châteauneuf-du-Pape

Grapes: Syrah, Mourvèdre, Grenache, Carignan, Viognier

Wine styles: Big, luscious red wines; rich, fruity whites; honeyed, cloying sweet wines.

Price range: Everything from cooperative-produced entry-level wines, to high-end blockbusters that will dent a serious hole in your wallet.

10. Sicily, Italy

Sicily is awash with incredible microclimates for quality wine-making. Volcanic soils, proximity to the cooling Mediterranean Sea and an array of wild herbs and various flora that give unique characters to the local wines. This is an area that is u-turning from previous factory-made wines to quality-driven wines today.

Wines: Nero d'Avola, Grillo, Marsala

Grapes: Nero d'Avola, Nerello Mascalese, Grillo, Catarratto, Inzolia

Wine styles: Big, luscious, warm reds; crisp, aromatic whites; honeyed, sweet wines.

Price range: Bargain-basement to medium price. Possibly one of the most value-driven regions for quality wine in Europe.

Vintage

The term 'vintage' simply refers to the year the grapes were harvested. It is generally displayed on the front label of the bottle. What is so interesting about the quality of the vintage is that it is wholly dependent on Mother Nature. If she plays ball and you have favourable growing conditions throughout the year, you will have a very successful vintage, meaning healthy vibrant grapes and brilliant wines, with wide critical acclaim. If the weather has been unpredictable, with freak storms, late frosts, heavy hail or burning hot temperatures, this of course will affect the quality of the fruit and the volume of the fruit produced. So naturally wine critics are very interested in judging wines and reviewing the success of each vintage the wine is produced in. Climate change is having a severe impact on the success or downfall of each vintage, and with this comes even more inclement weather and ultimately greater risks for winemakers. The difference in price in higher-end wines from vintage to vintage can vary massively. For example, a bottle of Château Mouton Rothschild, Pauillac, Bordeaux 1981 is €431. And the exact same wine is €1,436 for the 1982 vintage.

That's almost three times the price. This is simply because the weather conditions in 1982 were near perfect, with a mild winter, fresh spring, long warm summer and a dry harvest. In fact, 1982 is one the most iconic vintages in history. In high-end, long-established wine regions wine critics look at the success of the vintage and add that into their appraisal of the wine. Other iconic vintages are 1945, 1970, 2009 and 2010 in Bordeaux, and 1961, 1990, 1995 and 2010 in Burgundy. There are many, too many to list each region, but if you are hoarding wines and you are unsure if the vintage is good or not, there are many sites to check the success of the vintage, especially widely distributed sites like Wine Enthusiast, Decanter or Wine

Spectator. Generally, there are charts and guides per region to help steer you in the direction of the best vintages to buy and store, or indeed sell on.

It must be said, though, that for the majority of the wines that you or I drink from the shop shelves, the vintage is less important. If the winemaker is producing a wine to drink straight away there will be less concentration on tannins, oak ageing, lees ageing, bottle ageing or any other expensive technique that may be used to enhance the wine to last longer. Vintages are only really significant when we are in the realm of fine wines that are laid down to rest and enjoyed several years later. For the likes of our cheeky little Picpouls or our midweek Albariños, these are made to drink immediately so the importance of the vintage in question lessens.

Chapter 2

The Four Ss of Wine Tasting

On a random dreary day in Sydney, I arrived in for my Monday-evening shift at the restaurant and the sommelier was standing there with a kettle in his hand. Now, he was a quirky guy at the best of times, but standing at the entrance of a fine-dining restaurant with a kettle in your hand was just a touch weird, even for him. I had minus energy for doing anything that didn't involve lying on my couch and gobbling up mindless television, which is the sole purpose of a dreary Monday.

I shuffled on by him, put my bag away and got ready for my shift. His overzealous enthusiasm was already driving me crazy.

However, little did I realise that I would leave my shift that evening completely invigorated and totally blown away.

Mr Enthusiasm gathered us all over to practise sensations in our palate. We tasted several wines in our training session, but each was preceded by a hot drink, a piece of lemon, a dab of sea salt and a squeeze of toothpaste. Well, let's just say that, by the end, there was pandemonium in the galley. We howled and squinted and panted and cajoled. It was a life lesson in priming our palates.

First, we tasted a Chardonnay and a Pinot Noir before and straight after a sip of strong tea. It was incredible to see the marked difference between the two samples. The first sip was fruity and fresh, the second was bland and nondescript. The heat of tea will subdue your tastebuds, leading them to pick up far fewer flavours.

The fresh wedge of lemon was the best craic. The squints and squeals were a little gratuitous. But, to be fair to Mr Enthusiasm, after we licked the lemon and tasted the red wine, it was extraordinary – the wine became smoother, fruitier and juicier. We just couldn't believe it. We kept going back and trying it again. It was so cool to taste the differences.

We then proceeded on to the salt test with a white wine. What was interesting about this was that we had incredibly low expectations of this test. But the improvements from just a dab of salt were astonishing. It also created a fruitier wine, giving a far more intense presence in the mouth. It was like the salt was opening up our tastebuds. We all agreed this would be such a fun activity for a dinner party. The toothpaste was sadly what we expected. An abomination of the palate. Destroys all hope of any wine flavours making it through. The heat of the mint completely obliterated our senses. Not advisable at all.

But one of the best takeaways from a wine-training session like this was the power of combining ingredients and the ability of your palate to accept it – or not as the case may be. For us, it was such a fun way to learn about our palates and where you taste what. You should definitely try the salt and lemon test on your next gang of wine pals and just watch their faces – great craic.

Part of my wish in writing this book is so that you can teach yourself how to taste wine properly. Possessing the skill of tasting helps you judge wine on the spot – knowing the difference between a good-quality glass of wine and a glass of absolute turpentine. It will ultimately save you a fortune on drinking poor-quality wine

This tasting skill enables you to choose far better wines in the supermarket for your everyday 'at home dining experiences'. You start to recognise the regions and grapes you've tasted that appeal to you, therefore making future selections easier. And once you figure out the wines you like and understand why you like them, you will build up a veritable catalogue of your favourite wines.

Learning to taste wine consists of using three main senses – sight, smell and taste. But it's important to make sure that these senses are clear and heightened before you begin your tasting journey. What I mean by this is that before you set about tasting wine, clear your nose, don't wear perfume or use hand cream, don't use toothpaste directly before you taste, and steer away from curries, cigarettes and even powerful soda drinks, as these can all alter your tongue and tastebuds.

If you're at home and cracking open a bottle of wine of a Friday evening, do take the time to really taste it so that you can decide whether you like it or love it – think about what you like about it and then take note of the grape variety and the region of origin.

If you want to get really serious about it, take yourself off to a quiet, bright room and take your time to examine the wine.

In the next few pages are four pillars that will help break down the wine you're tasting to show you clearly where the wine may be lacking or not. This is a tried and tested approach I use called the 'Four Ss of wine tasting' – sight, smell, sip and savour.

Top tip
When tasting wine remember what you have consumed beforehand and how it may be affecting your palate. Curry, toothpaste, any mints, cigarettes and even a common cold all change your tasting abilities.

Sight

Firstly, it is important to look at the colour of the wine. The colour can tell us so much. It will indicate if the wine is ageing or not and it can help us to see if there's a fault in the wine. Before we get into the colour of the wine, it is crucial to give you an understanding of how much we taste with our eyes before we taste with our mouth and nose.

There have been many studies to assess the power of what we see and how it determines what we taste. Charles Spence of Oxford University claims that the taster's perception of the wine is dominated by what they see. Studies have shown that if we are looking at a bright-orange drink, and it is reasonably sweet and has a little acidity, we will categorise it is as an orange-flavoured drink – even if it is coloured apple juice.

A study conducted by a French PhD student in 2001 tested this theory on fifty-four top-end wine experts by adding dye to white wine to make it appear red. All the wine experts got it wrong. They described the wine as having the same attributes as a red wine. This study further validated scientists' claims that the brain processes olfactory (taste and smell) cues ten times more slowly than sight. Therefore, most of us already assume what the wine will taste like before we sample it. So, sight is key! Based on studies like these, winemakers realise the importance of producing crystal-clear wines that are appealing to the eye.

Colour

When judging the appearance of wine, the colour can tell us quite a bit – especially in reference to each style of wine as a standalone choice over time. Technically, we have four styles under different colours: white, red, rosé and orange. Examining the appearance and, more specifically, the colour of the wine can give us some indicators towards its taste and quality. If I had a euro for every person that commented on the golden colour of an oaked Chardonnay or an inky-black Spanish Monastrell, well, I would be sunning myself somewhere very glamorous.

To examine the colour properly, tilt your glass to a forty-five-degree angle and hold it over a piece of white paper – you should see the full, round circumference of the wine. This (where it touches the glass at the edges) is what we call the rim of the wine. The key is looking for a difference in colour between the centre of the liquid and the rim of the liquid. If the rim of the wine is paler, the wine is starting to age (discussed in more detail on p.49). Ageing will alter the quality of the wine, whether good or bad. Generally, basic everyday wines are ready to drink so ageing isn't a good sign, whereas your more expensive wines are intended to age.

Over time the colour naturally begins to fade. So as the colour lessens, it is the rim of the liquid where you can see this the most. This is a handy tip when judging the quality and the age of the wine. Try and see if there is a difference in the rim of the liquid as you tilt it, and does the colour get deeper as you look at the centre of the liquid.

How they achieve the colour in wine is related to the length of time the crushed grapes stay in contact with the skins.

- **White wine** White grapes are used and there is barely any skin contact at all – maybe an hour or two.
- **Orange wine** Whites grapes are used and the skin contact time can vary from twelve hours to a week.
- **Rosé wine** Red grapes are used and usually the skin contact is about twelve to sixteen hours.
- **Red wine** Red grapes are used and the skin contact can vary from twenty-four hours to two weeks (or indeed months), depending on the style of red required.

Within these four colours are variations again.

When looking at the colour of the wine, there can be a broad spectrum of white, rosé, red and gold colours. For example, a white wine can range from almost water-looking liquid (Pinot Grigio) to a yellow-coloured liquid (an oaked Californian Chardonnay) and everything in between. The colour will be determined by the length of time on the skins, but also by the initial colour of the skin of the grape. Some reds are light, pale and ruby-coloured (Fleurie) and this may be due to the short skin maceration time, but also the colour of the pale skin on a Gamay grape. In comparison to this the black skins of the Shiraz grapes give wines plenty of colour, even though the skins may only have been leaching in the colour for a shortish time. But the general point is that each grape has a different colour to their skin, and they're loosely categorised in these colours. It is helpful for you to consider though that it is both the colour of the grape skin and the length of maceration that lead to the end colour in the wine.

The very colours of the wine within the glass are important to help you judge the age of the wine also. Often, you will see a red wine turning slightly different tones of colour in the glass. A deep-purple wine will develop into a ruby colour, and then a ruby-coloured wine will develop into a tawny (brownish) colour, and so on. If you see a very pale-looking ruby or brownish colour, you know the wine is well into its ageing process.

With white wines, there will be a development of colour as the wine ages. We see this a little less because we tend to drink white wines when they are a lot younger. Nonetheless, if a white is ageing, it will develop from pale-lemon tones to deep-golden or orange tones. Ageing a wine can bring caramel, nutty notes. The youthful fruit in the wine will develop into dried fruits, and the colour will change from a bright, sparkling tone to a muted, golden hue.

The addition of oak ageing will also give a deeper yellow colour, as the oak imparts colour, but also as the wine ages, it intensifies in the barrel, therefore the colour will also intensify.

There is a craze at the moment for orange wines, mostly driven by hipster wine bars and those that prefer a weightier, grittier white. Orange wine is made from white grapes that have been crushed and have spent a longer time in contact with the skins. This longer skin contact gives a deeper colour to the white, a richer body to the wine and some grippy tannins.

Tannins are found in the skins of the grape, so if the flesh is soaking up these tannins, this will translate into the wine in the glass. Typically, tannins are less desirable in white wines, but if the producer is looking to age the wine, there may be a presence of tannins in the younger wine. But these will fade away as the wine ages in the bottle as the winemaker provisioned for. As always, remember you can soften these tannins by decanting your wine and giving it some air. These wines are not for the faint-hearted and are meant to be consumed with food – and rich foods at that.

Clarity

In today's extremely demanding world, the general consumer tends to look for wines that are clear and bright in appearance.

During the winemaking process, wines are clarified and filtered. Various techniques are used to remove all the micro-scopic elements, like particles of the grape skins, pips or yeasts.

If you see a haze in your wine, chances are the wine producer is a natural winemaker. These winemakers avoid fining (see next page) and filtering as they believe this draws out too much of the flavour and soul of the wine. So, the finished wine looks a little cloudy as all these particles are still floating in it. Even though cloudiness is not technically a fault, this style of wine is the least visually appealing to the general public. Also, just to note, the cloudiness does not affect the flavour of the wine. You will be surprised by the freshness of these wines. Be brave and sip away.

Crystals and sediments

Looking at the wine will also help you to discover if there are tiny crystals or sediments. These crystals are formed when naturally occurring potassium and tartaric acid react and form on the bottom of the bottle cork. The crystals can drop from the cork into the wine through motion and vigour and can end up in the bottom of your glass. Although this is less of a problem than it has been previously, it still occurs. To be honest, crystals are pretty harmless but, again, they can play havoc with your senses and lead you to think that the wine is flawed.

Sediments are also naturally occurring tiny deposits that occur during the winemaking process. They are broken-down yeast particles that fall to the bottom of the barrel after fermentation and ageing. These minute particles can often be removed from the liquid using a method called racking, where one barrel is tipped into another, making sure the larger particles are caught in the neck of the first barrel and are therefore not transferred into the second. Furthermore, winemakers will use a gelatinous agent during the fining process to draw the microscopic particles to the bottom of the next barrel with ingredients such as egg white, fish bones or milk proteins or a type of clay called bentonite, which wine producers add to produce a vegan wine.

Top tip
Always remember if you see these tiny little particles
in your wine, the easiest way to remove them is to
tip your glass of wine gently into another, trying your
best to gather the sediment slowly up the glass as you
tilt it over. You can also get a decanter and pour the
bottle slowly into the decanter at a forty-five-degree
angle. Decanting is discussed further in Chapter 6.

Smell

If I told you that we taste over 80 per cent with our noses, would you believe me? Think back on the times when you've had a cold, or worse still Covid, and you've lost your sense of taste because your nose was blocked. It is a such a strange sensation to chew food and taste nothing. I absolutely dread when this happens. The joy I experience from different flavours, and more so mixing these different flavours together, is just precious. We're a far cry from the days of boiling the bejaysus out of a side of ham, mixed with pale-green, tasteless cabbage and maybe a few blanched white spuds – foods that have as much flavour in them as a sheet of white paper. How we survived overboiling the life out of anything on our plates, I'll never know. Today, tasting good-quality food and drink is almost a national sport for us.

Enhancing your taste experience with smell

The tongue is an incredible organ. It has tastebuds all over the tip that are filled with ten to fifty sensory cells each. But without our sense of smell, our taste sensations are limited to the five basic taste qualities: sweet, salty, sour, bitter and umami. (Umami describes flavours associated with characteristics of meatiness, cheese or soy, and is particularly present in red wines that have had a long fermentation.)

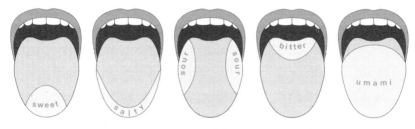

Taste areas of the tongue

Every other flavour we taste is from our sense of smell. So, every time you pick up a glass of wine, give the wine a good swish or swirl and have a sniff. If you are smelling aromas such as green apples or peaches or perhaps some oak, this will be the result of the vapours that have travelled from the glass to your nose. As you lift the glass to take a sip, keep smelling these aromatic vapours as the liquid gushes into your mouth. The vapours will travel down the back of your nose and down your throat to where the olfactory nerve is located. This connects your sense of smell and taste.

The olfactory nerve then sends impulses to various parts of your brain, telling you what you are tasting. Combined with the five tastes you experience from your tongue, the extra vapours achieved from swirling your wine make for a far greater taste experience. Hence the energetic swirling that wine nerds like myself are a big fan of.

Try it yourself the next time you pick up a glass of wine. Try tasting it without swirling and then taste the wine after you have given it a generous swish, and notice the difference between the two sips.

A good swirl in the glass immediately awakens the volatile compounds, which are the organic compounds in the wine that have a high vapour content to them. You could also say that they are the exciting parts of the wine: the aromas and the alcohol. The aromas are stuck in liquid form initially, and it is the action of adding air to the wine that frees them in the glass and into your nose.

Generally, an excessive amount of swirling goes on in any professional wine tasting. Sometimes, you wonder if there will be any wine left. But the science behind it justifies the embellishments.

Checking quality by aromatic value

When you smell wine, not only are you improving your taste sensation, you are also determining the quality of the wine. Generally, a wine should have a fruit-driven smell. Even novice tasters can pick up aromas of green apples, strawberries, mangoes, etc. However, the real value lies in deciphering whether the fruit aromas smell real or fake. Think of real, freshly picked strawberries compared to the Starburst version of strawberries.

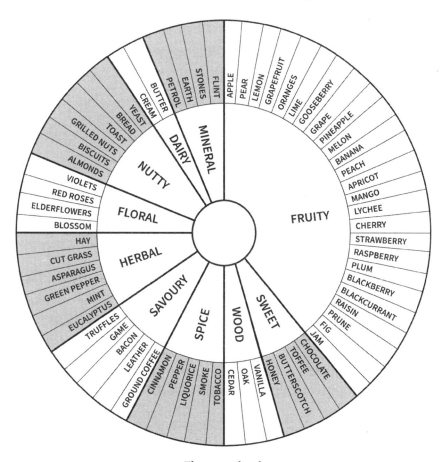

Flavour wheel

If you are put on the spot in a restaurant and asked to judge the quality of the wine, the first thing you should do is check the fruit aromas. Does it smell like freshly picked fruit or does it smell like a packet of sweets a ten-year-old child would salivate for? This is a foolproof method for checking for quality. Factory wines will have sugars added to them during the winemaking process as the fruit quality is poor and does not have enough natural sugars to raise the alcohol levels – this gives the wine that exaggerated aroma of sweets. And there is just no comparison to the real thing.

I remember tasting a very expensive Burgundy Pinot Noir for the first time – the bottle cost €500 and this was back in 2002! Myself and my fellow wine nerds clubbed in together to buy the wine and this particular gaggle got less than a quarter of a glass each. However – and I pause when I say this – it is still to this day one of the greatest epiphanies I have ever had when tasting wine.

We waited with bated-breath on each sip and each comment from our wine expert, who guided us through this taste sensation. The fruit we tasted in this wine, even though the wine was eight years old, was akin to freshly picked fruit. Just the right amount of sweet and sour you would expect from your favourite strawberry from Wexford. It was extraordinary. I realise that, for most people, this experience would pale in comparison to watching the Northern Lights or completing a marathon, but, to a wine nerd like myself, it was close. I tasted grilled mushrooms in the wine. I tasted old leather, mixed beautifully with crushed blackcurrants, hints of violet flowers and a sprinkle of baking spices on the finish. The wine looked pale, but it was creamy and silky in my mouth. If I'd closed my eyes, I would have felt like I was swallowing a delicately flavoured yogurt. It blew my mind. This is the ethereal magic of Pinot Noir grown in near-perfect soils that create a shooting star like this. It is a day I'll never forget.

Layers of aromas – how to find them?

Part of wine tasting lies in the skill of fine-tuning your nose to pick up all sorts of subtle aromas. This might sound like the oddest of skills but, really, it's about being present in the moment.

I always recommend you take the time and start practising to smell your food, perfume and the smells at the beach, in the park or even the diesel you put in the car. Basically, you are training your nose to pick up more than one aroma. You're looking – or should I say smelling – for sweet aromas, spiced aromas, savoury aromas or chemical-based aromas. When you start to recognise some of these aromas, you can add them to your memory bank.

For example, German Riesling will often develop a petrol tone in its aged versions. People always stare at me blankly when I say this. This aroma comes from a unique flavour compound that is naturally found in the Riesling grape. The slate soils found in the Mosel Valley are an active vehicle (pardon the pun) for the promotion of this particular compound. When these grapes are fermented, it helps to draw out these compounds and so, as the wines age, they tend to soften into oily-like aromas. When you smell a distinctive Riesling like this and experience the oiliness, your mind will be blown too.

Corked wines

Another major benefit to taking your time and smelling your wine is being able to identify corked wine. There are many misnomers that circle the industry today, but corked wine is when the cork in the bottle has been attacked by a fungal virus. This attack can occur in the cork tree itself, when the corks are being made or even when the cork has been placed in the bottle itself. This fungal attack cannot be prevented despite major research into it.

To be honest, the smell from corked wine is like an old wardrobe from the 1980s. Worse still, like those horrific mothballs your granny would leave in the wardrobe to ward away those pesky little moths. The smell would knock you out – and that's how corked wines smell.

Interesting fact for you, the human nose is so sensitive to TCA (trichloranise), which is the compound produced by this mould, that we can smell a teaspoon amount in an Olympic-sized pool. It is caused by an age-old battle between plantae and fungus to be very exact for your next dinner-party trivia session!

Here are a few basic facts if you come across a wine that smells like your granny's wardrobe:

- If you think you can smell an off odour, the chances are the wine is well underway to being corked.
- You can drink corked wine and it will not make you sick. However, the grim aroma will consistently travel up your

nose while you are drinking, and it will make for a rather poor wine experience.

- If your wine is corked, you can return it straight away to your waiter or, indeed, to the store you bought it in. The shop that sold you the wine does not lose out; the onus falls upon the wine producer, who foots the bill for the faulty wine.

- About 3-6 per cent of all wines using wooden corks suffer from this naturally occurring fault. Despite all modern research, it is still impossible to curb this phenomenon.

- If the wine is sealed with a screwcap, the percentage of damage and fault is less than 1 per cent. For these wines however, one of the tiny catches can break and extra oxygen will get into the bottle, causing the fruit flavours to disappear. The wine will lack vibrancy and will seem exceptionally sour.

Sip

Sight and smell are not enough to determine a wine's quality. As the old phrase goes 'the proof is in the pudding'. Tasting the wine is an essential part of this complete sensory experience.

Further to just tasting the wine in your mouth, the fundamental key to checking the quality of the wine on your palate is adding air to your sip. The 'reverse whistle', as described by Jancis Robinson MW (Master of Wine), enables you to take even more air into your mouth to further open out the aromas.

As the wine rolls around your mouth, you are looking to judge the acidity levels, the variety of the flavours, the weight of the wine and its length or finish, amongst many other features. Truly we could dissect the wine so brutally it becomes a liquid of broken parts and, to the untrained palate, makes no sense. Therefore, it is best to stick to four key indicators to check for quality:

1. **Acidity** This is found at the sides of your tongue. If the acidity of a wine is overly aggressive, the idea of chewing a lemon will be preferable! A good wine should mellow out with the joy of the ripe, sweet fruit flavours in the mid-palate.

2. **Weight** To judge the weight of the wine, let it caress your tongue and see if it resembles a watery texture or if it has a fuller, creamier mouthfeel. This should indicate its richness and full-bodied character. Understanding the weight of the wine helps you gauge what you are in the mood for. Do you crave a light and refreshing white or are you in the mood for a rich, soft, jammy red? Weight in itself is not an indicator of quality, but if a wine is *too* light and lacklustre in flavour, it has most likely come from bad quality grapes.

3. **Flavours** Layers of flavours are a true sign of quality. Of course, the winemaker wants you to taste the character of the grapes, but they also want to you to taste the addition of oak ageing, or lees ageing (which I discuss in more detail on p.178) or blends of grapes, and whatever extra flavours they choose to add. So have a little think about it. Are you smelling fruits, spices, flowers or pastry or all the above? Furthermore, do the flavours taste real? Much like the smell, check and see if the flavours taste fresh and like real fruit and not the confected, sweet version of the fruit.

4. **Length** This is probably the best indicator of quality. The longer a grape hangs on a vine, the longer it will collect extra nutrients and flavours. Perfectly ripe grapes with longer hang time mean less manipulation in the winery and, ultimately, give longer lasting flavours. A quality wine should linger in your mouth for thirty seconds to a minute. A very good-quality wine will last longer. A cheap and poorly made wine will have no flavour after you swallow the wine. It will vanish.

It's extraordinary: as soon as you start to notice these seemingly subtle differences, you realise that they tell you so much. The finish is a foolproof way to check for quality in a wine.

Savour

Savouring your wine may be one of the most important parts of wine tasting. When we imagine the romanticised notion of a winemaker spending hours in the vineyard growing the perfect fruit, they don't have in mind me and my girlfriends swilling the wine down in crappy glasses with a load of crushed ice. These grapes are their babies and they have invested many months in them – pruning, shading, fertilising, picking and crushing – all with love in mind.

Recently, it struck me that most of the wine tasting I do for my job is drinking wine in a mindful way. I take time to slow down, find a quiet spot, swirl my wine and allow myself to slip deep into thought about the various aromas and flavours of the wine before making my assessment. All carried out in a peaceful, serene, reflective manner.

Of course, tasting wine is not about practising mindfulness. It is the systematic method in which wine is judged. Its purpose is to effectively homogenise a very subjective subject. But the two worlds – mindfulness and wine assessment – go together well and, without one, we can't have the other.

Enjoying wine is a whole other exciting matter that we have down to a fine art. It's the tasting and assessment that take some time to master. Wine is made to reflect the land and all it has to offer, so time and patience are needed to master your wine skills.

Foolproof indicators of quality wine:

- **Clean nose** Not corked or oxidised
- **Fruit aromas** Smell like real fruits, not confected versions
- **Many different aromas** Fruits, spices, earthy tones, floral tones
- **Feels balanced** Feels like a perfect orange that is sweet and refreshing
- **Finish** The wine has a long finish and you can taste it after swallowing

Chapter 3

Grape Expectations: What to Expect from Your Favourite Grape

Did you know?
Wine grapes and snacking grapes are different!
Many new wine drinkers don't realise that the
grapes used to make wine are not the same grapes
that we buy in the shops to eat! They have many
considerable differences - from skin thickness to
sweetness and even the grapes' size. The big takeaway
is you definitely will not be making good-quality wine
from grapes from your local shop: the flavours from
those grapes would be bland, watery and bitter.

Now that we have begun to taste wine in a more conscious way, the next step in being able to mindfully and confidently choose wine that you know you're going to like is getting to know your grapes.

Grapes are the gateway to knowing the flavours in a wine. I clearly remember arriving back from Australia, and taking a job with this amazing guy who was the Rhône Valley specialist in Ireland at the time. I learned so much from him about full-bodied, juicy red wines based around the Syrah grape.

Syrah is a big, beautiful, silky, aromatic red wine with flavours of violet flowers and white pepper. It is a wine that endears itself to you instantly. Shiraz is Syrah's big, bulky cousin, whose grapes have spent time in the sun and so are overripe with a remarkable spiciness. Are they the same grape? . . . The simple answer is yes.

Was I afraid to ask this simple question? . . . The simple answer is yes.

It's one of those questions that seem glaringly obvious, but, in fact, there is always an element of doubt to most things we think are a given. So, I actually didn't ask my boss at the time, but I used the training that I had received in Oz instead.

Like the good wine nerd that I am, I tasted each wine slowly and carefully. I checked the fruit in the wine and what the flavours could tell me. The Syrah seemed fresher, like a tangier fruit. Yes, there were dark berries, but they felt slightly under-ripe with higher acidity.

Then, I tasted the Shiraz.

The fruit I tasted in the Shiraz were like overripe blackberries. Like they had been left in the sunshine on your kitchen window-sill before you ate them. Whereas the blackberries in the Syrah were like they'd been taken straight from the bush and they still need a little resting time. Yes, both wines had spices in them but, again, the Syrah's spices felt sharper and tangier, like a white pepper. The spices in the Shiraz felt warmer and rounder, like a crushed black pepper.

The last difference was the mouthfeel. The Syrah felt slightly silkier, with a smoother feel; the Shiraz felt grippy with bigger tannins and an all-round bigger feel in the palate. Because the annual weather is slightly cooler in the Northern Rhône, Syrah here tends to have less sugar, therefore a lighter feel on the mouth. Shiraz is basking away in the Southern Australian sun, and so the sugars increase, and so does the alcohol content. This leads to a weightier wine due to these surplus glycerol-type sugars. I was chuffed that I was able to distinguish between them without any help. Tasting the wines side by side made all the difference.

Also, when trying to figure out the grape, think about the climate of the country it came from. France is warm in the summer, even hot, but the winters are cold and the spring is unpredictable. Compare this to the long, baking-hot summers in Barossa Valley, a warm, sometimes hot, autumn, a mild winter and a reasonably warm spring. Sugar levels and therefore alcohol levels will be higher in warmer climates.

Top tip
It's so interesting to taste wines side by side. It gives you a comparison point to work with and the contrasting flavours will help to highlight the differences clearly.

So, let's get cracking.

Would you believe me if I told you there are over 8,000 grape varieties in the world today? Imagine walking into your local supermarket and trying to choose between 8,000 styles of wine. Oh, sweet lord. It's bad enough with over 200 classified styles of wine in our shops, ranging from light, zippy low-alcohol Vinho Verde to a full-bodied, rich Amarone at 16 per cent alcohol – and everything in between.

When considering the world's most popular twelve grape varieties, it is interesting to note that these take up a third of the vine area of the world, according to the International Organisation of Vine and Wine (OIV). This is not because of a lack of grapes to choose from, but primarily because of familiarity.

The rest of the world is covered with lesser known vines that may have slightly less commerciality to them – so their flavours appeal to a far smaller audience or there is a degree of difficulty to cultivating them or, indeed, they have lower sugar levels that deem the grape lower quality. It is far easier to sell a wine with recognisable grape names like Cabernet Sauvignon, Chardonnay, Sauvignon Blanc and Pinot Grigio.

Furthermore, these grapes are considered a safer bet in non-native lands – they are either French or Italian, but have the ability to grow well in Australia, New Zealand or America. Many wineries succumb to the pressure of mass media, and use these more reliable grape varieties that are the safe bet viticulturally – and financially – but are less authentic to their region.

However, there are a few countries that have a rich diversity of local vines and, thankfully, some producers have chosen to stick to their local varieties. Spain, Greece, Germany and Austria are certainly known for sticking to their own local grapes, that grow best in their soils with their climate. Their culture and heritage have taught these producers to keep to their own native vines as these also require less fertilisation and less manipulation, therefore give a cleaner, more authentic fruit and, of course, wine.

There has been a big trend in many wine-producing countries in the past ten years to use indigenous grapes. They are a far more sustainable option, requiring fewer chemicals to grow. They are also higher in quality and uniqueness.

Another such country is Italy, which has a treasure trove of indigenous grapes. Its most-planted variety, Sangiovese, which makes Chianti, does not exceed 8 per cent of the country's total vine area because they use their indigenous grape varieties in greater number than any other European country. Italians have an established wine culture and have been using their own vines since the Roman era. Much finesse and development has been put in to finding the right site, the right soil and the right microclimate for these indigenous vines to thrive.

Producers are often scared to put lesser-known grape names like Assyrtiko or Pecorino or Grillo or Vuira on the label, as they feel they won't sell. But I promise you, if you tasted these wines as a lover of Sauvignon or Chardonnay, you would be instantly impressed.

In New Zealand, one variety – Sauvignon Blanc – represents 60 per cent of the country's vine area. In France, the most-planted grape variety is Merlot and it covers 14 per cent of the country's vine area.

In the USA, the two most-planted grape varieties are Chardonnay and Cabernet Sauvignon, and they cover 10 per cent and 9 per cent, respectively. Tempranillo is Spanish, but probably more famously known as the principal grape of Rioja in northern Spain. Along with Airén, it is very dominant in Spain. They are planted on almost 45 per cent of the Spanish vineland.

Among the top twelve grape varieties in the world, there are many so-called international varieties. These are French but are so ubiquitous that people often forget they're French and so they get called international instead – they include Pinot Noir, Sauvignon Blanc, Merlot, Chardonnay and Cabernet Sauvignon.

Much of the planting of French vines was also down to the reverence people had for French wines as a whole. When wine producers in California, Australia and New Zealand truly began their crusade for a modern wine industry in the 1970s and 1980s, French wines dominated the global market. Between 1990 and 2016, the plantings of French vines was nearly double that of Spanish and Italian grapes.

Added to the reverence of consumers and producers for French wines, Italian and Spanish varieties tend not to thrive as well in other countries. This could partly be because they're relatively new to these countries and need time to settle, but they aren't as marketable as the big giants and so are harder to sell to new and eager wine growers looking to make money.

Origin of grapes

Like any other plant in the world, grapevines began as wild, untamed greenery. They grew all over the Middle East and, over time, as winemaking developed, the male plant and the female plant were propagated to create a hermaphrodite. This is the vine that is considered most 'fruitful', pardon the pun.

From ancient references back in 5000 BCE of wild vines across the area that is now Georgia, Russia and Iran to modern-day examples of European vines that grace our shop shelves, the *vitis vinfera* vine has had a long and illustrious history. This is the variety of grape we use to make quality wine, which has been chosen because of its exceptional longevity and genetic makeup.

This history has allowed the vine to cross breed and mutate inextricably over time, which has led to a gargantuan array of unique and fascinating vines for winemakers to work with. There has also been vast manipulation and hybrid breeding of grapes in nurseries all over the world.

What we think of as a simple Sauvignon Blanc might have four different French clones and the likes of Pinot Noir might have over a thousand! These different clones have varying idiosyncrasies, such as mildly different flavours or a better ability to withstand certain weather conditions.

In layman's terms, they are the Rolls Royce of fruit to ferment and make an alcoholic drink from. They have the highest sugar content – and sugar is what is converted into alcohol in the fermentation process. Of course, you can make wine from many other types of berries. In Ireland, wine is made from blackberries and strawberries. You can also make wine from apples, pears or even a pineapple if you wish. But the *vitis vinifera* vine is the chosen one because of its generous levels of sugars, acids, tannins and natural yeasts. Wines made from other fruits generally require added sugars or acids or, indeed, added flavours.

The aim of quality winemaking is to achieve perfectly ripe fruit so you have less manipulation in the winery. The humble grape delivers on ripeness and character, which other fruits often lack.

Anatomy of a grape

A grape is essentially a berry. Clusters of berries are attached to the vine by a stem. The most important parts of the grape are the skin, pulp and the seeds.

- **Skin** This consists of ten layers of waxy cells that are waterproof. They also contain the colouring matter – red or yellow pigments – aromatic compounds (some of these compounds give the grape their distinct flavour), tannins, antioxidants and potassium. Anthocyanins are the pigments that are responsible for the red and purple colour of the grapes.

- **Pulp** The pulp is located below the skin layers of grapes. It contains sap or juice that, when pressed, is called the free run. Within the pulp of the grapes are acids, sugars, aroma compounds and water.
- **Seeds** These are localised in the centre of the grape and float in the flesh. They are filled with tannins, which can be useful for red-wine production.

Inside of a grape

Flavours

If wine is made from only grapes, how does it have all the various other fruit aromas and flavours?

This is possibly one of the most frequently asked questions I get. And that's totally fair enough. You often see descriptors of red wine talking about strawberries or raspberries, or white wines mentioning gooseberries and green apples. What's going on? Are they adding these fruits in to achieve these flavours? Amazingly, the answer is no, and that is possibly one of the most fascinating things to learn about wine.

So where do the flavours come from?

The flesh of the grape consists of sugars, acids and these flavour compounds – the matter in the grape that has an odour. Without getting too technical, these compounds are known as volatile aroma compounds. They are small molecules that easily turn into a vapour and reach our nasal cavity when we smell or drink a glass of wine (as mentioned on p.53).

Each grape variety has its own unique selection of aroma compounds. During fermentation, these flavour compounds are brought to life. When the fermentation heats up, this creates new chemical compounds. These new compounds are said to be the exact same aroma compounds found in green apples, strawberries, raspberries, etc. Essentially, the fermentation process changes the muted aroma compounds to flavours we can smell, taste and recognise.

Basically, when a reviewer or taster is picking up a strawberry aroma, they're literally smelling an exact strawberry-flavour compound.

Without being too cheesy about the whole thing, this is genuinely 'where the magic happens'. Fermentation brings a simple grape juice to an alcoholic liquid, but also discovers unearthed and hidden flavours in these high-quality grapes. Astonishing stuff really. The fermentation is drawing out these flavours from the grapes through heating up these compounds that are found in the flesh of these supremely high-quality grapes. There's no added flavours here, just simple chemical reactions that bring to life this organic matter.

Characteristics of grapes

It is estimated that twelve grape varieties make up 80 per cent of wine production, and another 138 varieties make up a further 19 per cent of production, meaning 99 per cent of wines produced are made from 150 grape varieties. And now that we know how these extraordinary flavours are brought about, by the quality of the grapes and the fermentation process, let's have a look at some of the most popular varieties in today's market.

Here is a list of the most widely grown and globally produced wine varieties consumed in the world:

1. **Cabernet Sauvignon** 840,000 acres (340,000 hectares)

2. **Merlot** 657,300 acres (266,000 hectares)

3. **Tempranillo** 570,800 acres (231,000 hectares)

4. **Airén**, primarily used for Spanish brandy, 538,700 acres (218,000 hectares)

5. **Chardonnay** 518,900 acres (211,000 hectares)

6. **Syrah** 470,000 acres (190,000 hectares)

7. **Grenache Noir** 402,780 acres (163,000 hectares)

8. **Sauvignon Blanc** 299,000 acres (121,000 hectares)

9. **Pinot Noir** 285,000 acres (115,000 hectares)

10. **Trebbiano Toscano/Ugni Blanc**, primarily used for brandy and balsamic vinegar, 274,300 acres (111,000 hectares)

11. **Riesling** 120,000 acres (48,700 hectares)

12. **Zinfandel/Primitivo** 71,000 acres (28,732 hectares)

From this list, I have chosen the top ten varieties that are consumed and enjoyed here in Ireland. Further to this, I have added another three popular grape varieties that are widely sold and enjoyed in Ireland.

For a bit of craic, I will try and explain the grape varieties like someone you might know in your life. Learning the characteristic of these grapes will help you remember what you like and, ultimately, help you choose better wines the next time you're in the shop. (FYI – you'll see the term 'aged flavours' on the following pages. This refers to the flavours that develop in a wine over time.)

I have chosen not to concentrate on Trebbiano or Airén, which are the main grapes found in Italian and Spanish table wines, respectively. Instead, I have chosen to concentrate on the most popular grapes consumed in Ireland.

Grape	Who	Flavours	Aged Flavours	Structure
Cabernet Sauvignon Origins: First discovered in Bordeaux, France.	This is your big, burly, gym-loving, brash friend. In your face but in a good way.	• Blackberries • Black cherry • Plums • Damsons • Pencil shavings • Tomato leaf	• Cigar box • Dried toast • Leather • Pencil lead	• Big tannins in youth • Full body • Dark fruits • Medium-plus alcohol

Where Grown	Climate	Foods
Primarily Bordeaux, France. California and Australia for serious quality.	• Needs plenty of sun – loves a warm, temperate climate. • Excessive heat in Chile or California will create high-alcohol and jammy flavours.	The strong tannins are brilliant with hard cheeses and the sinew in red meats. Ideal with roasted lamb and braised meats.

Best Buys

A *Steal* – affordable Bordeaux, Lacombe Cadiot

A *Splurge* – Stags' Leap, Napa Valley

Grape Expectations: What to Expect from Your Favourite Grape

Grape	Who	Flavours	Aged Flavours	Structure
Merlot Origins: France, Bordeaux specifically.	The outgoing, caring friend, who is soft, tender and vivacious.	• Blackcurrant • Black cherries • Figs • Plums • Damsons • Liquorice	• Sandalwood • Tobacco • Truffle • Mushroom • Cinnamon • Nutmeg • Toasted almonds	• Soft tannins • Soft, rounded mouthfeel • Medium-plus body • Medium alcohol

Where Grown	Climate	Foods
Now grown worldwide, very adaptable grape. Best affordable versions are from Chile and Australia.	Loves warmth, but not too hot, so, the alcohol levels are never crazy high.	Best served with red meats, casseroles and hard cheeses.

Best Buys

A *Steal* – Chilean Merlot from Tupungato, Domaine Bousquet, Merlot from south of France

A *Splurge* – Château de Sales Pomerol, Bordeaux

Grape	Who	Flavours	Aged Flavours	Structure
Tempranillo (aka Cencibel/ Ule de Lebre) Origins: First discovered in northern Spain.	This is your bubbly, outgoing, confident and smooth-talking friend. Always reliable.	• Strawberries • Red cherries • Raspberries	• Coffee bean • Dried fruits like raisins and dates • Nutmeg • Vanilla • Coconut	• Soft, rounded mouthfeel, with smooth but present tannins • Medium weight in body • Medium alcohol

Where Grown	Climate	Foods
All over Spain, mostly Rioja and Ribera Del Duero. Also in Portugal.	Plenty of warm sunshine but can be sensitive to sunburn. Needs a cold winter to lengthen this early ripening grape.	It's quite the seasonally affected grape, so a warm climate will produce a darker version that's great for steak and a lighter red-berry version is beautiful with roast lamb.

Best Buys

A Steal – Rioja Joven level, Yecla, Alicante and La Mancha in Spain, 1605 Tempranillo

A Splurge – Pingus, Ribera Del Duero

Grape Expectations: What to Expect from Your Favourite Grape

Grape	Who	Flavours	Aged Flavours	Structure
Chardonnay Origins: Chardonnay is the love child of Pinot Noir and Gouais Blanc, which was created by the Romans in eastern France. This is where the world's best Chardonnay is produced.	This is the aunt who loves a good Chanel two piece, with a drowning of perfume, and is the last to leave a party. She will flourish anywhere.	The flavours are very dependent on where it's grown. Cooler climate: • Green apple • Mineral freshness Warmer climate: • Pears • Grapefruits • Honeydew melon	Aged in oak: • Butterscotch • Biscuits • Honey • Buttered toast • Candyfloss	Cooler climate: • Lighter body • Higher acidity Warmer climate: • Higher sugar levels • Richer wines • Often oaked to enhance flavours

Where Grown	Climate	Foods
This grape grows everywhere, but thrives in France, New Zealand and California.	In cooler regions, this grape will produce wines that are steely and brimming with green-apple acidity. In warmer climates, it will produce wines that are super ripe and bursting with fruit flavours.	Because of its diversity it can pair with a whole range of foods, specifically white meats, raw fish and creamy pastas.

Best Buys

Burgundy Chardonnay is the best but very expensive.

A *Steal* – Limoux in the south of France, Domaine Begude Etoile Limoux

A *Splurge* – Domaine Jean-Louis Chavy Puligny-Montrachet

Grape	Who	Flavours	Aged Flavours	Structure
Syrah/Shiraz (same DNA in these grapes) Origins: Syrah was originally discovered in the Rhône Valley, France. Shiraz has travelled to Australia and South Africa.	Syrah is your brooding, strong and handsome friend who likes to play rugby. Shiraz is a similar friend but is tanned and loves American football.	Syrah: • Red cherry • Violets • White pepper Shiraz: • Blackcurrants • Black pepper • Plums	Syrah: • Earthy tone • Sweet tobacco • Leather Shiraz: • Prunes • Mocha • Sweet vanilla	Syrah: • Rich, round mouthfeel • Silkiness Shiraz: • Weightier body • High tannins • High alcohol

Where Grown	Climate	Foods
Widely grown. Europe and Old World for Syrah. Australia for Shiraz.	Absolute sun worshipper, so loves warmth and sunlight. Needs a cooler winter to slow down the ripening cycle to get better flavours.	Northern Rhône Syrah goes well with game, venison and beef. Sun-kissed Shiraz goes with BBQ meats, and charred, roasted red meats.

Best Buys

A *Steal* – Le Pinede Costières de Nîmes, a region for value-driven Shiraz; Bethany First Village Shiraz

A *Splurge* – Stefan Ogier Côte-Rôtie (Syrah); Henschke Mount Edelstone (Shiraz)

Grape Expectations: What to Expect from Your Favourite Grape

Grape	Who	Flavours	Aged Flavours	Structure
Grenache Noir Origins: It is believed this grape originated in northern Spain.	This is your elegant, but fierce bestie who exudes a wildness and vivaciousness and wears plenty of perfume.	• Strawberries, like deliciously sweet, canned strawberries • Raspberries with a dusty tone	• Leather • Roasted nuts • Honey • Gingerbread	• Lighter colour • High acidity and generous alcohol • Juicy and mouth-filling red

Where Grown	Climate	Food
This heat-loving grape grows all over Spain and the south of France. Famous for being the main grape in Provence rosé.	Adores the sun, but producers must be careful of the excessive sugars turning into high-alcohol wines. Needs to be handled carefully.	This medium-bodied red suits lighter meats like turkey, chicken and pork. Goes fantastically well with vegetarian pasta dishes.

Best Buys

A Steal – Spanish Garnacha from Navarra for cool-climate flavours, e.g. Le Naturel Garnacha

A Splurge – Château Rayas Châteauneuf-du-Pape

Grape	Who	Flavours	Aged Flavours	Structure
Sauvignon Blanc Origins: believed to have been first discovered in Bordeaux. Its homestead is the Loire Valley in France.	This is your girly pal who's a bit of a livewire. Can be feisty and prickly, but generally full of joy and presence.	Underripe flavours: • Granny Smith apple • Lime • Kiwis • Green peppers In warmer regions: • White peach • Nectarine • White melon	Not really known for its ageing potential, so it rarely is. However, when blended with Sémillon, it takes on flavours of: • Guava • Pineapple • Boiled sweets	• High acidity • Light mouthfeel • Refreshing and racy

Where Grown	Climate	Foods
One of the most widely grown white grapes in the world. It is very adaptable and will grow in a whole host of countries.	Because of its cool-climate origins, it tends to fare better in cooler regions. This ensures the flavours stay fresh and green, as classic Sauvignon Blanc should be.	The natural high acidity in this grape is one of its best features. It cleanses your palate easily after a creamy cheese or creamy pasta dish. It is also a wonderful companion to asparagus and aubergine.

Best Buys

A Steal – Touraine, Loire Valley, Guy Allion Touraine. Or for Marlborough New Zealand try Astrolabe

A Splurge – Comte Lafond, Sancerre, Loire Valley, or Cloudy Bay, New Zealand

Grape Expectations: What to Expect from Your Favourite Grape

Grape	Who	Flavours	Aged Flavours	Structure
Pinot Noir Origins: One of the oldest cultivated vines in history, that started its illustrious life in Burgundy. This long-aged grape is one of the healthiest to drink with high levels of antioxidants in the skins.	This is your well-educated friend, who possesses a quiet confidence. A sleek, charming and timid character.	• Fresh strawberries • Raspberries • Red cherries • Think summer red berries, with a hint of wild herbs	When aged gracefully: • Leather • Woodsmoke • Boiled cabbage (a desired yet subtle flavour)	• Uniquely beautiful pale-red colours • Juicy • High acidity gives a refreshing mouthfeel

Where Grown	Climate	Foods
Burgundy – few places can compare to the heights of Pinot here. Oregon in the US and New Zealand are certainly creating fine, more value-centric Pinot Noir.	Unbelievably difficult to grow this grape that likes a cold winter to hibernate. The vine needs a mild spring without frost as this can destroy the buds. A warm summer will help to ripen the berries. But not too warm, as this can quicken the ripening process, making fewer interesting flavours.	Earthy flavours like mushroom and game are synonymous with the Burgundy region. The high acidity in Pinot Noir will also slice easily through fatty meats like duck or goose.

Best Buys

It is no secret in the wine world that Burgundy Pinot Noir is extremely expensive and often overpriced.

A Steal – Geil Trocken, German Pinot Noir

A Splurge – David Moret Rully, Burgundy

Here are a few more grapes that are commonly seen on shop shelves in Ireland.

Grape	Who	Flavours	Aged Flavours	Structure
Pinot Grigio (Pinot Gris) Origins: Originally a grape discovered in Burgundy. This is a mutated version of Pinot Noir.	This is the giddy young sister to your well-educated Pinot Noir friend. She's the one at the back making faces and generally having the craic.	• Yellow apples • Honeydew melon • Fresh pear	Pinot Grigio (skilled producer, with low yields): • Stone fruits • Amalfi lemons Pinot Gris (superior French grape): • Wild honey • Rhubarb • Spiced tea	Pinot Grigio: • Light-to-medium body • Cleansing finish Pinot Gris: • Weightier • Better intensity of interesting flavours

Where Grown	Climate	Foods
Veneto, in the north-east of Italy. Unfortunately, Italian wine laws are not as strict as their other European counterparts. With a gap in the market for a style of white that is aromatic with gentle acidity, the Italians decided to capitalise on this and completely overcrop this grape.	This grape needs a long, cool winter and a warm, long ripening summer. Pinot Gris is certainly a far cry from the often over-produced, watery Italian versions that flood the market. When Pinot Grigio is over-cropped it leads to a very watery appearance to the wine.	Parma ham, blue cheese and salad work well with good-quality Pinot Grigio. A bland cracker will work well with the godawful over-cropped Pinot Grigio that can dominate the shelves. Pinot Gris works well with quiche, bacon, salad and some ripe peaches.

Best Buys

A *Steal* – Regions like Veneto and Sicily are making everyday styles

A *Splurge* – San Simone Pinot Grigio, Friuli, Trentino-Alto Adige, or Zind Humbrecht Alsace (Pinot Gris)

Grape Expectations: What to Expect from Your Favourite Grape

Grape	Who	Flavours	Aged Flavours	Structure
Malbec Origins: commonly considered Argentinian, but in fact it originated in south-west France, near Bordeaux.	This is your gym-loving friend who loves their muscles, but also loves a good festival in the sun. Sun and fun is Malbec's favourite duo.	Malbec wines tend to be deeply coloured and have super-ripe flavours with soft tannins: • Dark berries • Damsons • Plums • Cocoa beans	• Old leather • Dark fruit • Violets	• Soft and plummy • Rounded, pleasing mouthfeel

Where Grown	Climate	Foods
Malbec began to thrive on the slopes of the Andes, in well-drained soils and a semi-Mediterranean climate. One of the main hotspots for quality-made Malbec is Mendoza.	It thoroughly enjoys the extended warmer sunshine hours, giving a softer, riper style than its reserved French cousin.	The wines made from these sun-drenched grapes love a good ribeye steak, roast leg of lamb or even a dark chocolate souffle.

Best Buys

Best versions are from Mendoza (Argentina) and Cahors (far more rustic style from France).

A *Steal* – Catena is an excellent value-driven Malbec from Mendoza

A *Splurge* – Staying in Mendoza, Pulenta Estate, Gran Malbec

Grape	Who	Flavours	Aged Flavours	Structure
Albariño Origins: primarily associated with the Rías Baixas region in north-western Spain, particularly in Galicia. Also grown in Portugal, where it is known as Alvarinho.	This is the livewire bestie who dreams of long, warm nights in Ibiza, fuelled with hyper juice and a sprinkle of glittery happiness. And of course, a pink cowboy hat for good measure.	• Pineapples • Mangoes • Yellow apples • Lime peel • Salty notes	Not really known for its ageing potential. Aged versions are rare but brilliant: • Lemon • Lime • White flowers • Honey golden	• Golden colour • High acidity • Weighty mouthfeel • Rich mid-palate

Where Grown	Climate	Foods
In Galicia, to overcome hardy weather conditions the grapes are grown on pergolas. This format creates a wind tunnel to dry the grapes, but also keeps the grapes off the wet ground and prevents rot.	Galicia experiences 2200mm of rain a year, and here in Ireland we experience 1600mm. The excessive rain also helps to create a high level of acidity. Many of the local vineyards are close to the sea, leaving a salty residue on the skin of the grape.	Goes exceptionally well with all types of fish. The high acidity acts like the wedge of lemon, and the saline character is like the seasoning. This wine will also pair well with smoked, cured meats, like chorizo, and hard cheeses, like Manchego.

Best Buys

Best-value versions can be from northern Portugal, known as Alvarinho. There are varying degrees of quality of Albariño, but in Galicia there is quality across the board.

A Steal – Alvarinho in Vinho Verde, Quinta de Soalheiro

A Splurge – Ribeira Sacra, Domino do Bibei

Grape Expectations: What to Expect from Your Favourite Grape

Grape	Who	Flavours	Aged Flavours	Structure
Nero d'Avola Origins: Native to Sicily in Italy, it is widely cultivated and has become one of Sicily's signature grape varieties. Of late it has flooded restaurant wine lists and shop shelves due to its fruit-forward nature.	I can hear the chitarra playing in the background watching this suave and extremely tanned yet slightly rustic Italian gent cruising around the place. Cool personified.	• Dark berries • Black cherries • Plums • Blackberries • Dried fruits • Black pepper • Thyme • Liquorice	Typically created to be enjoyed in its youth with a soft fruit-forward appeal. With age: • Black coffee • Roasted Brazil nuts • Cocoa	• Thick, dark skins, contributing to the wine's deep colour • Fleshy mouthfeel • Soft fine tannins • Generous weight

Where Grown	Climate	Foods
As well as Sicily, also grown in Puglia, Sardinia (Italy), Australia.	Warm temperatures and long sunshine hours are preferable. Sicily is the island of baking sun, volcanic soils and cooling sea breezes, so vines are happy as clams here. There are some Australian examples, but they generally don't shine like their Sicilian counterparts.	Goes exceptionally well with Italian dishes that contain ragu-style meats. Hard cheeses are also a classic pairing. Look to the traditional dishes of Sicily too: grilled cutlets with local herbs, Arancini balls or some pasta with sardines.

Best Buys

Sicily is known for its value-centric wines. The level of quality for the price is almost unrivalled anywhere in Europe. It is classed as a high-value, high-quality region.

A *Steal* – Da Vero Biologico Rosso, Sicily

A *Splurge* – Most are less than €20 but for a little something more special head to Terre Siciliane, like a Cento Cavalli

Grape	Who	Flavours	Aged Flavours	Structure
Riesling Origins: This German-bred white grape is considered to be the 'Queen of white grapes'. When grown on slate soils, the acidity levels elevate.	This female goddess of a white grape plays the cello, speed reads, cycles a unicycle with ease and is a wiry Pilates queen. Perfection is life for this lady.	Over 70 per cent of German Rieslings are fermented dry. Flavours include: • Citrus fruits • Peach • Apricot • Ginger • Honey • Rhubarb • Toffee apple • Petrol • Beeswax	• A petrol or oily aroma unique to this style of wine	• Mouth-tingling acidity • Gum-cleansing minerality • Acidity and structure allow it to age for fifty years plus in high-end wines

Where Grown	Climate	Foods
In Germany, wines have naturally high acidity due to colder winters and lesser sunshine hours so if sugar is added in post-fermentation, this style of wine is called a 'Liebfraumilch', direct translation being 'milk of our lady'.	Germany is on the cusp of the latitude band that deems vine growing possible. It has long cold winters and long Indian summers that extend the length of time the grapes hang on the vine, allowing the flavours to develop. This is the jewel in the crown for the stunning grapes that grace the German slopes.	Riesling is known for its piercing acidity, ideal for cleansing your palate after a bite of rich seafood, pâté or cured meats. Riesling works well with roasted pork, and if the wine has a little sweetness, pairs nicely with spicy foods.

Best Buys

Germany is the home of Riesling, but you can also source some fine examples from Alsace in France and Clare Valley in Australia.

A Steal – Mosel Valley in Germany. Even the cheap wines here are cracking – Dr Loosen Riesling

A Splurge – Mosel Valley but higher up the slopes with a producer like Scharzhofberger

Rosé

It would be a crying shame if a book about wine and all its charms did not include the eponymous rosé wine that is made from red grapes but has a peachy-orange colour.

What was once considered a bit of a naff wine back in the 1980s and 1990s has now had the biggest glow-up in the wine world imaginable. Thanks to the likes of big names such as the infamous Whispering Angel and Miraval (owned by Brad Pitt), rosé is gracing the terraces of many a city around the world.

It is hard to define the origins of rosé, as many red wines were a pale colour in the early days of production. It is believed, though, that the Phoenicians circa 500 BCE brought their vines into the south of France, namely Provence. And they began to ice down their wines and dilute them slightly to create a lighter, newer style of wine. These settlers mainly concen-trated on local grapes like Grenache and Syrah. Grenache is now considered one of the finest grapes for rosé production. Its thinner skins and juicy, flavourful flesh are ideal for making these elegant pale-coloured wines that are adored the world over.

How is it made?
The flesh of red grapes is transparent and so the flesh is left in contact with the skins for twelve to twenty-four hours, depending on the producer. In red-wine production, grapes are fermented with the skins; in rosé the grapes are fermented without the skins - exactly like white-wine production. This

creates a lighter style of wine from a red grape that has fewer tannins and less colour, but plenty of flavour and aroma.

The production methods can vary slightly. Some producers will choose the 'press' method, where the grapes are immediately pressed after being picked. The juice leaving the press encounters the skins and picks up a slight hue. This creates a far lighter pink colour.

The 'saignée' method – it means 'to bleed' in French – is where grapes are left on the skins for up to twenty-four hours. This is the more common method. When the grapes are put in the tank, they break under their own weight and the juice mixes with the skins within the tank. After a period, the juice is drained and will have a slightly deeper colour than when the press method is used. This maceration production style is most used in the south of France, Spain and Italy.

In post-Covid Ireland, rosé consumption has steadily increased from 5 per cent to 7 per cent. It is unequivocally associated with summer – which is when I drink it. It has the perfect balance between a chilled white wine and a richer, fuller red wine.

One of the most important factors defining the rise of rosé has to be social media. Whispering Angel is owned by the son of a Russian businessman, who was an esteemed wine producer in Bordeaux before they set their new site on a sunny hill in Provence. When they moved, they brought with them big pockets and, most importantly, big dreams of a quality-driven rosé that was based on the premise of a Bordeaux châteaux. The quality is there, but their relentless marketing through product placement in affluent areas like the Hamptons, Cannes,

Nice and Cape Cod has created the dream-lifestyle wine that people aspire to drink. Like them or loathe them, you cannot take away from their marketing prowess.

Some of the most common grapes used for rosé production are Grenache, Sangiovese, Syrah and Pinot Noir. The most popular style of rosé is the Provençal style, which is pale salmon in colour, and usually light with flavours of grapefruits and red berries.

Top tip
The colour of the rosé does not determine the weight of the wine. Often people assume the paler the colour the lighter it is, but the colour is down to the thickness of the grape skins and how long the wine has spent on the skins when crushed.

Blended wines

When we see more than one grape on a label of a bottle, it is called a blend. There are many styles of wines globally that are blended wines. Some of the most famous examples would be wines from Bordeaux (Cabernet Sauvignon, Merlot and Cabernet Franc), wines from Côtes du Rhône (Grenache, Syrah, Mourvèdre) or wines from Valpolicella (Corvina, Molinara, Rondinella).

Blending is an age-old winemaking technique that has been practised for hundreds of years.

Using a number of grapes enables the winemaker to fine tune the wine. Grapes have different defining characteristics, and these come in handy for perfecting a blend. For example, in marginal regions where weather can deeply affect a crop, such as Bordeaux, using a blend of grapes provides an insurance policy year in, year out. Some grapes are late harvesting and if the weather has been unkind, these will not fare well. Other grapes are durable and hardy and will survive the climatic issues. Therefore, a careful blend of these grapes can help create a more consistent style for the producer each year.

There are other reasons you might blend:

- Changing the flavour of the wine by using more expressive grapes.
- Changing the structure of the wine by using grapes with higher tannin levels.
- Balancing the oak with the use of grapes that favour oak better.
- Highlighting certain plots of your vineyard by using grapes that fare better here.

See the tables on the following pages for some more examples of famous blends.

Wine blend	Grapes
Châteauneuf-du-Pape Rhône, France	• Grenache • Syrah • Mourvèdre • Bourboulenc • Cinsault • Clairette Blanche • Counoise • Grenache Blanc • Muscardin • Picardan • Piquepoul Blanc • Roussanne • Terret Noir • Vaccarese
Red Bourdeaux France	• Merlot • Cabernet Sauvignon • Cabernet Franc • Petit Verdot • Malbec
White Bordeaux France	• Sémillon • Sauvignon Blanc • Muscadelle
Red Bourgogne France	• Pinot Noir • Gamay
White Bourgogne France	• Chardonnay • Aligoté

Wine blend	Grapes
Red Rhône/GSM France, USA & Australia	• Grenache • Syrah • Mourvèdre • Others
White Rhône France & USA	• Marsanne • Rousanne • Viognier • Clarette • Grenache Blanc • Bourboulenc • Others
Soave Veneto, Italy	• Garganega • Terbbiano • Chardonnay • Pinot Blanc • Others
Chianti Tuscany, Italy	• Sangiovese • Cabernet Sauvignon • Cabernet Franc • Others
Super Tuscan Tuscany, Italy	• Merlot • Cabernet Sauvignon • Sangiovese • Syrah • Cabernet Franc • Others

Grape Expectations: What to Expect from Your Favourite Grape

Wine blend	Grapes
Amarone della Valpolicella Veneto, Italy	• Corvina • Molinara • Rondinella • Others
Rioja Spain	• Tempranillo • Mazuelo (Carignan) • Graciano • Maturana Tinta
White Rioja Spain	• Viura (Macabeo) • Malvasia • Verdejo • Garnacha Blanca • Others
Priorat Spain	• Grenache • Syrah • Carignan • Cabernet Sauvignon • Merlot
Meritage USA	• Cabernet Sauvignon • Merlot • Cabernet Franc • Petit Franc • Malbec • Carménère

Wine blend	Grapes
Port Duoro, Portugal	• Touriga Nacional • Touriga Franca • Tinta Roriz • Tinta Barroca • Tinta Cão • Others
Provence Rosé France	• Cinsault • Grenache • Syrah • Rolle (Vermentino) • Others
Champagne France	• Chardonnay • Pinot Meunier • Pinot Noir
Cava Spain	• Macabeo • Parellada • Xarello • Chardonnay

Field blends - originally popular with the Greeks and the Romans - are making a comeback. They were an extended array of different types of grapes grown in one field to help alleviate the vulnerability of each growing season in terms of unpredictable weather. It was a bit of a case of 'throw enough mud at the wall and something will stick'.

As research and development took over in the wine world,

vine growers became more adept at choosing better sites and soils for their very unpredictable crops. So single varietal grapes were all planted together. These are some of the recognisable images we see of manicured rows and rows of perfectly groomed vines.

A field blend is the complete opposite. Nature is allowed into the field. For centuries, this is how grapes grew. At harvest, the interplanted grapes are picked and fermented together. This is a risk, as some of the grapes may not be fully ripe and they may have different fermentation properties, but adventurous natural winemakers are trying their hand at this ancient method of vine cultivation.

They are the distant footprint of the terroir and the skill of the winemaker. Vienna in Austria is a city that is home to many of these field-blend producers on the outskirts of the city. Conscientious natural wine-makers are creating some amazing wines here. There are a very small number of talented winemakers that are producing field blends in Alsace and Douro Valley.

Non-alcoholic wines

There has been an unprecedented appetite for non-alcoholic drinks with the rise of a growing demand for healthier lifestyles. The global market for non-alcoholic wines has ballooned rapidly, with world sales estimated to be worth around $1.6 billion. This section of the wine industry is projected to grow by 7 per cent by 2026 compared to its position in 2022, making it one of the fastest growing sectors of the wine market. Spirits and beers have spearheaded the non-alcoholic drinks surge, with high-quality offerings to consume. So, the wine industry has had to take note and join the party. The Wine Paris trade show, one of the most important events in the sector, devoted a significant part of its 2024 exhibition space to alcohol-free wines. Renowned producers seized the opportunity to showcase their innovative creations and meet a growing demand.

Non-alcoholic wines have been typically made using traditional winemaking methods, i.e. the grapes picked, crushed and then fermented. This is then followed by a delicate and precise dealcoholisation process, such as vacuum distillation or reverse osmosis. This removes the alcohol while retaining the flavours and aromas. Basically, the wine is spun so fast that the alcoholic vapours rise. These vapours are then trapped in a separate column or glass container, leaving a wine with remnants of the original wine. Unfortunately, once you remove the ethanol (alcohol compound), this will mute the wine somewhat, as ethanol is the magical component responsible for expressing aromas and flavours in the wine. Some producers may add some grape must (the first press juice), which is sweet and unctuous. This is used to replace the glycerol body of the missing alcohol. There is no denying this is a difficult process that produces wines that often lack the very heart and soul of the wine. But such is the stage we are at in the work of non-alcoholic winemaking. Wine is a far more delicate liquid than spirits or beers, therefore the differences in the non-alcoholic versions are far more obvious.

There are some keen winemakers around the world attempting to make some reasonably well-made versions. Producing a non-alcoholic red wine is more difficult, as when you remove the alcohol, this can highlight the bitterness and the tannins. Bubbles in a wine help to mask the dumbed-down flavours. Some grapes are better at retaining flavours after the de-alcoholisation process. Therefore try and stick to white grapes like Riesling or Albariño or else sparkling for non-alcoholic wines.

Try:
- Hollow Leg, Albariño, Spain
- Leitz Eins Zwei Zero, Riesling, Germany
- Freixenet Legero Sparkling, Spain

To conclude, the study of wine grapes includes a myriad of factors that influence the final character of wine, including grape variety, climate, region and winemaking practices. The flavour and structure of wines are ultimately shaped by these elements, with each grape offering incredibly unique aromatics and flavour. The key is figuring out which suits you best. Regions like Bordeaux, Burgundy and Tuscany are known for producing some of the world's best grapes, mainly due to their ideal growing conditions and centuries of viticultural expertise. However the world is witnessing a rise in excellent quality grapes found in so many new and exciting regions, and we the congregation of wine lovers are the luckier for this.

Top 150 Grape Varieties

1. Cabernet Sauvignon
2. Merlot
3. Tempranillo
4. Airén
5. Chardonnay
6. Syrah/Shiraz
7. Garnacha/Grenache
8. Sauvignon Blanc
9. Pinot Noir
10. Trebbiano/Ugni Blanc
11. Riesling
12. Zinfandel/Primitivo
13. Barbera
14. Sangiovese
15. Malbec
16. Chenin Blanc
17. Viognier
18. Gewürztraminer
19. Moscato/Muscat
20. Nebbiolo
21. Cabernet Franc
22. Pinot Grigio/Pinot Gris
23. Carménère
24. Petit Verdot
25. Gamay
26. Touriga Nacional
27. Albariño
28. Grüner Veltliner
29. Sémillon
30. Verdejo
31. Torrontés
32. Aligoté
33. Mourvèdre/Mataro/ Monastrell
34. Petite Sirah/Durif
35. Lambrusco
36. Fiano
37. Marsanne
38. Roussanne
39. Vermentino
40. Cortese
41. Glera/Prosecco
42. Viura/Macabeo
43. Cinsault
44. Tannat
45. Blaufränkisch/ Lemberger
46. Aglianico
47. Nero d'Avola
48. Assyrtiko
49. Xinomavro
50. Mavrodaphne
51. Pinotage
52. Dornfelder
53. Silvaner
54. Gros Manseng
55. Furmint
56. Kadarka
57. Zweigelt
58. Saperavi
59. Rkatsiteli
60. Carignan/Mazuelo
61. Trousseau
62. Teroldego
63. Refosco
64. Negroamaro
65. Bombino Bianco
66. Dolcetto
67. Brachetto
68. Cesanese
69. Montepulciano
70. Frappato
71. Nerello Mascalese
72. Prugnolo Gentile
73. Verdicchio
74. Pecorino
75. Bombino Nero
76. Falanghina
77. Biancolella
78. Greco
79. Lacrima
80. Nosiola
81. Raboso
82. Rossese
83. Susumaniello
84. Valpolicella/Corvina
85. Gaglioppo
86. Kerner
87. Freisa
88. Schiava
89. Erbaluce
90. Timorasso
91. Vernaccia
92. Malvasia
93. Vidal Blanc
94. Baco Noir
95. Norton
96. Frontenac
97. Seyval Blanc
98. Traminette
99. Maréchal Foch

Other varieties contributing to 99% of wine production:

100. Arinto
101. Antão Vaz
102. Vinhão
103. Encruzado

104. Baga
105. Alfrocheiro
106. Aragonez
107. Trincadeira
108. Castelão
109. Rabo de Ovelha
110. Perrum
111. Síria
112. Loureiro
113. Alvarinho
114. Azal
115. Avesso
116. Cainho
117. Rabigato
118. Viosinho
119. Moscatel
120. Touriga Franca
121. Tinta Barroca
122. Tinta Roriz
123. Tinta Cão
124. Alicante Bouschet
125. Moscatel Galego
126. Bical
127. Maria Gomes/
     Fernão Pires
128. Sercial/Esgana Cão
129. Terrantez
130. Verdelho
131. Malvasia Fina
132. Bual/Boal
133. Tinta Negra Mole
134. Rainha Santa
135. Amaral
136. Bastardo
137. Baboso
138. Listán
139. Marufo
140. Rufete
141. Cerceal
142. Donzelinho
143. Sercial
144. Sercialinho
145. Verdelho Tinto
146. Alvarelhão
147. Camaraou
148. Complexa
149. Samarrinho
150. Sezão

Chapter 4

Sip and Symphony: The Artistry and Abomination of Winemaking

> *Did you know?*
> *In the sixteenth and*
> *seventeenth centuries, French winemakers added*
> *lead to their wine barrels, which would dissolve into*
> *the wine, imparting a luscious sweetness that captivated*
> *the tastebuds. It seemed like a stroke of genius. However,*
> *as more people indulged in these sweetened wines, a*
> *silent epidemic began to spread - lead poisoning.*

It was slap bang mid-Celtic Tiger era in Ireland and I'd been back from Australia for a couple of years. And I'm keen to remind people of the absolute vulgar insanity that went on in the restaurants of Dublin at that time. Corporate credit cards were ripped asunder. Manners and general decency were out of fashion, and entitlement and tackiness were in. I have many a tale to tell.

I spent most of my twenties and some of my thirties travelling and working as a waitress. Why? Because being a waitress in the 2000s meant accessible money, experience in the hospitality industry and a wide gaze into the human behaviours during this heady time for Ireland. Throw excessive alcohol levels into the mix, and this leads to some fine tales indeed. A veritable social study if ever there was one. It was an exhilarating and fascinating time, and the stories are endless.

However, there are a certain few that come to mind.

I was standing at a table taking the order of seventeen rugby fans or, as they are commonly known, 'rugger buggers'. It was becoming a tedious task because the Lansdowne boys had plenty of pints of Guinness on them at this stage. The chatter was rapid and the 'ya ya, greeeeaaaat's were flying. I was getting a bit bored to be truthful. But money seemed to be no object and tips were my lifeblood, so the wry smile was a permanent feature on my face. As I completed my escapade around the table, I finally reached the last more-than-merry punter. I would have described him as delicately inebriated. In another realm, I would be referring to him as a pain in the backside. He was loud, lairy and just ever so obnoxious. As I took the wine order from him, I remembered I had a half-eaten Cadbury's Caramello in the kitchen to polish off. *Oh, hurry up,* I thought to myself. Out of nowhere, he orders two bottles of Prosciutto to start and two bottles

103

of Château de Mouthwash for their mains. Well, I giggled the whole way back to the kitchen, and not because he got the names wrong. That's easily done. But because he was so jarred that what he called them could never have passed as the original names: Prosecco and Château de Mouton Rothschild. Everyone else was so ballooned at the table, they never even realised their supposedly capable friend was ordering bottles of Prosciutto and Mouthwash. From those days onwards, those wines would forever be known at that restaurant as such. Good times.

Now, to be fair to this excitable and rather drunk young man, mouthwash does have alcohol in it – some mouthwashes even contain more alcohol than wine, averaging around 10 per cent ABV (alcohol by volume). Some Listerine products have a whopping 26.9 per cent alcohol, which is a higher alcohol content than found in most beers, most wines and even some digestifs. So perhaps he had consumed a Château de Mouthwash at home. You should, however, note that the alcohol found in these mouthwashes has been treated with other chemicals and isn't intended to be drunk. The sole purpose of mouthwash is of course to rinse your mouth and nothing else. Scary but true that household items can have that level of alcohol in them. Meanwhile, back in the land of giggles, the lads ended up being very sound. We had a great laugh through the night, and, of course, I did let him know by dessert the choice collection of names he had used, and he burst out laughing.

Suffice to say, the days of the Celtic Tiger are well behind us now, and we have been through some tough times economically. We all want the best bang for our buck, and that often means a delicate balance between quality and quantity.

While a night like this is gas and a funny story to be told, truthfully these guys were a little too drunk to really *taste* the wine that night. Point being, remember your audience and your setting. If you have had far too many shandies, spending your hard-earned money on quality wine could be the biggest waste of your money ever.

Quality levels and how they vary

Much like many food items, wine has become an industrialised product. For many wines, it is less about the foot treading and green pruning, and more about the million-gallon tanks that hold the wine. Poor-quality wines will have a general confected nature about them. The flavours and the aromas will be a heightened sweetish version of the fruits in the wine, and the colour can often look a little off, maybe a bit unnatural due to the addition of colourings. The finish on the wine will be non-existent and the intensity of flavours is usually very low. It feels like a watered-down version of a wine you actually enjoy.

There are some wines that resemble a mild glass of mouthwash, and there are wines that will blow your mind. So how can we tell the difference? Bottles of wine can vary in price from €7.50 to €650,000 per bottle. How can we tell if the wine inside is worth the same as a postage stamp or a hefty mortgage? So many questions to answer and so many answers to give.

This is the chapter where we sift through the wine industry. And we'll look at the most important factors, after grapes, that affect the taste and quality of the wine – how large corporate entities produce enormous factory-style wines, and how to steer clear of these. These wines become less about the quality of the fruit and the nature of the surrounding area, and more about the colossal revenue that can be achieved. Yes, there's a beautifully marketed story behind the brand, but there is little glamour in a factory that is producing 65 million cases a year, with machines that fill 58,000 bottles an hour. Meanwhile, there are smaller producers with very different production styles and very high quality wines to offer.

However, the real investigation lies in how wines differ if they are made by a massive machine or an artisan. Does the taste change?

How is the wine made?

To delve further into the difference between mass-made wines and smaller-producer wines, it's important to look at the production methods and, most importantly, the motivations of the winemakers.

On the one hand, wine is treated like a revenue-generating

commodity, created to make money and please a multitude. In this case, the wine drinker treats the purchase of mass-made wine like a grocery of sorts, like buying bread or fruit or sugar.

On the other hand, we have producers who are motivated by interest and quality, and a careful thought process is involved. These producers will take a little more time in their production and maybe a little exploration too.

So, for context, let's have a look at wine production and how it has evolved from the very beginning to where it is today.

When wine first began

As we discussed in Chapter 1, there is many a fable surrounding the beginnings of wine, but, truthfully, the most concrete evidence at the moment is that originated in Georgia. With the spread of viticulture, and farming in general, came the domestication of grapes and, as a result, a wine-drinking culture in the region.

At that time: 8000 BC
- Grapes were left to naturally crush in the jar.
- Wild yeasts react with the sugars in the grapes, creating the alcohol-laden berries.

As time went on: 5000 BC
- They moved from consuming alcoholic berries to eventually squeezing the juice into wine as we now know it.
- The berries were squeezed to release the juices, creating a finer, more delicate wine.

- Natural indigenous yeasts were still being used. This was a completely natural process using only environmental factors to aid grape growth.

From the sixth century BCE, the Greeks and Romans brought wine culture into their everyday lives – at a time when it was safer to drink wine than water. Time and money went into making the industry more sophisticated. Ingredients like herbs, honey, sea water and even lead were added to balance the overly tart wines and give them a boost.

Wines were used for medicinal purposes; they were deeply embedded within the Church and were copiously consumed within a social environment. This meant that production levels rose dramatically. The advances of proper site selection to improve the ripeness of grapes began around this time, and the Romans were famously known for introducing oak barrels for ageing their wines. They began to introduce wine to every part of their lives.

As time went on
- Studies were carried out to improve the site selection of the vineyards.
- Grapes were planted on south-facing slopes for more sunshine hours and better ripeness.
- Grapes were crushed in larger tanks that were far more controlled by the winemaker.
- Wines started to represent their local region (the notion of terroir – the natural environment where a wine is produced – began).

- Oak barrels were invented out of necessity for transporting the wine.
- Wines were unfiltered.
- Vintages were recorded and studied each year.

The only manipulation at the time was the addition of ingredients like honey, resins, sea water and lead. This time predates the use of chemical fertilisers, so the food chain of life was heavily relied upon for generous grape production.

Animals were used as natural predators within vineyards to prevent grape spoilage. Snails would devour the leaves of the vines, so frogs were introduced to consume the snails, which, in turn, would be preyed upon by snakes, and so forth. This was the natural life cycle to keep the vines free from predators.

The use of sulphur dioxide (SO_2) was first permitted in 1487 by a Prussian royal decree. It was first used by the English and the Dutch to retain freshness in wines when they burned sulphur candles in barrels before they were filled for long sea journeys. Sulphur dioxide is considered a relatively innocuous preservative agent that prevents oxidation and unwanted bacteria. It can also act as an antibacterial cleaning agent in empty tanks and barrels.

Just after the industrial revolution in the early twentieth century, the scale of winemaking became even larger again. The first-ever stainless-steel tank was created in 1928, but it really only hit the wine scene from the 1960s onwards.

Modern winemaking

Stainless-steel tanks enabled winemakers to take complete control of fermentation, a previously volatile process. Fermenting in a non-controlled tank made from wood or cement, as was used previously, was very difficult to control – temperatures would rise and the wines would spoil easily. The use of stainless steel meant temperatures could be completely controlled to dictate the flavour and the quality of the wine.

It also enabled winemakers to produce on a grander scale. It was the bereft dairy industry in New Zealand in the 1970s that spurred on this revolution in the wine industry. New Zealand had been left with thousands of empty stainless-steel tanks after trade deals collapsed with the UK. So, a new purpose needed to be found for them. The success of these tanks in winemaking spread globally. Million-gallon tanks, bottling lines, mechanical harvesters and clarification systems were created and the production of mass-made wines exploded.

- Grapes are now mass picked by machines that can work day and night.
- These machines have sorting tables on them that eject berries that are too heavy.
- Massive crushing and pressing machines in the winery further segregate unwanted berries to help ensure the style of wine required.
- Huge stainless-steel tanks are temperature controlled during fermentation.

- A further array of large tanks is now employed for clarification (filtering the wine).
- Depending on the style of wine, some of the juice will be oak aged in a variety of old or new barrels.
- Huge bottling lines are in operation to bottle the juice, label the wine and add the closure (cork or screwcap).

Since the 1960s, vine growers have been heavily reliant on chemical fertilisers, pesticides and herbicides.

Sulphur is still used throughout the winery as a disinfectant to clean the barrels and as a preservative to the wine just before it is bottled.

Further chemicals are added using food colourings, preservatives, confected sugars, tartaric acids and flavourings. Often mass-made wines will use cheap oak offerings like oak chips, oak powder or an oak stave in the middle of the tank in an attempt to replicate the taste of oak barrel ageing.

Modern wines are often made in pristine environments that resemble science labs. This is, of course, referencing the large-scale producer. There are still many smaller producers that are batch crafting, or indeed artisan crafting, their wines in small oak barrels, with time and love invested.

Like any spectrum in the world, there is every other type of producer in between. Medium-sized wine producers, those who are part of a local cooperative, lone rangers and every size in between. But let's stick with small and large for a moment.

Comparisons between a small and big producer

Business models

Big-brand wines

- Familiarity, especially the market of novice wine drinkers.
- Reliability of flavours, despite changeable weather each year, i.e. the Coca-Cola recipe never changes.
- Far greater volume of grapes required, therefore lesser quality fruit is used.
- Grapes are sourced from vast areas, sometimes covering half a continent.
- Cost of production is lower, and usually done on flat lands that are far cheaper.
- Machine harvesting and million-gallon tanks.
- Recipe-style wines that are made in the factory and not the vineyard.
- Excessive use of additives, colourings and flavourings to compensate for poor-quality fruit.
- Production volumes are predicted and met, despite possible climatic disasters.
- Heavily marketed (bright colours, recognisable labels) and widely distributed.

Small-producer wines

- Incredibly diverse and unique.
- Very often made from grapes in one vineyard or vineyards within a certain locality.

- The wines reflect the local climate, soils and culture.
- Production levels rely heavily on the weather of that vintage.
- Cost of land is usually higher.
- Higher cost involved using good-quality oak barrels for fermentation or ageing.
- Virtually no marketing whatsoever – they rely on wine critics and word of mouth.
- Availability can vary massively because of smaller production levels that are not scalable or predictable.
- Often there's less use of chemicals, including additives and added sugars.
- Generally, they are family run and often properties are handed down through generations of tradition.

Motivation of consumers

Big-brand wines
- Familiarity and ease of purchase.
- Speeds up the purchase as branded wines are often very conveniently placed.
- Builds a common ground with their peers who may also be familiar with the brand.
- Seeking a safe bet.
- Appeal to non-wine drinkers.
- Often consumed in an unconscious manner, i.e. big party or watching a movie.

Small-producer wines

- Consumer is looking to try something new.
- Consumer may be looking for a suitable wine to pair with a chosen food.
- Up for a greater thought process to choose a wine like this.
- Has the time to read producer information or wine-tasting notes.
- Consumer is looking for a wine that will have layers of flavours and complexity.
- These wines will often be consumed with a fellow wine enthusiast, and plenty of the conversation will steer towards the quality of the wine and the flavours being tasted.

Taste

Big-brand wines

- Simple, generic, pleasing flavours.
- Quite often confected sugars will be added to balance the lack of ripe natural sugars.
- Confected sugars will make the fruit aromas in the wine smell like sweets, rather than fresh fruit.
- The flavour intensity will be far less impactful.
- Usually there is one overriding aroma and flavour.
- The finish on the wine after you taste it is very short.
- When the bottle has been opened, the wine won't last forty-eight hours.

Small-producer wines

- Flavours will reflect the local climate, soils and winemaking heritage.
- Layers of flavours like fruit, floral, oak, spice and herbaceous notes will be found.
- Very often these wines will also have a textural appeal in the mouth, e.g. silkiness, weightiness, richness, dryness.
- Wines will be well balanced between natural sugars, natural acidity and alcohol.
- Best paired with foods, as they contain far less sugars than their mass-made counterparts.
- Often produced to age well, and therefore flavours will develop and become nuttier and creamier.
- The length on the finish is far longer, leaving a flavour long after the wine has been drunk.

The more complex and layered a wine is, the slower you drink it. It is to be sipped, savoured and pondered about.

Top tip
If your wine tastes of sweets and has that confected feel to it, chances are the wine is poorly made and is full of added sugars and flavourings.

Common additives used in winemaking

Additives are used in wine to enhance convenience, speed, production levels and, fundamentally, maximise profits. There are two generic groups of additives: common and corrective.

As the latter term implies, corrective additives are used to balance the wine in the winery. If you think about it from a very humble beginning, the aim of the winemaker is to create a wine from perfectly ripe grapes that have just the right number of balanced sugars and acids. Think of those times when you get that perfectly sweet yet tangy orange, which is as rare as hen's teeth. In an ideal world, quality wine is made from perfectly ripe grapes that need minimal intervention, or indeed corrective additives, in the winery.

Good wines can be made in the wineries; however, great wines are made in the field.

So, if you're making 58,000 bottles an hour on one machine within a huge winery, you can imagine the number of grapes you need to have. Statistically, around ten clusters of grapes make a standard bottle of wine. If you are gathering grapes from a variety of regions, and a vast terrain that differs in terms of sunshine hours, rainfall, soils and climatic conditions, the selection of the grapes will vary greatly. Some will be ripe, underripe, overripe, too small, too big . . . the list continues. With a cornucopia of grape conditions, these corrective additives help make the wine and balance the books. That said, many of these additives are harmless and, furthermore, have been used for centuries.

Sulphur

Sulphur is added to wine before and after fermentation. It is used to disinfect wine barrels and helps a wine retain freshness for many years. It gets a bad reputation, with many claiming their residual headaches from wine drinking are caused by the sulphites. Less than 1 per cent of the world's population is allergic to sulphur, and there is generally more sulphur found in a bag of dried fruits or Tayto crisps than in a bottle of wine.

Natural winemakers will bellow from the rooftops of the benefits of making wine with no sulphur at all. However, it requires a high level of skill from the winemaker to achieve a sulphur-free wine that does not have an earthy, mousey tone to it.

Sugar

The process of adding sugar to wine is known as chaptalisation. Sugar is not added to create a sweeter taste, but actually is used to bump up the alcohol level, sometimes by up to 3 per cent ABV!

In some wine-producing regions – like Australia, California and South Africa – adding cane sugar is not permitted. However, in regions such as Bordeaux and Provence, where grapes can struggle for ripeness and the acids are high, it is acceptable to add cane sugar. As mentioned, this will not make your wine sweeter because the sugars are gobbled up by the yeasts and converted into extra alcohol through fermentation. This process is primarily used in years where the sunshine hours and ripeness levels are majorly compromised.

It is important to highlight the high levels of added sugars that are in some of the mass-produced wines. But first I think I need to fully explain the difference between added sugars and natural sugars.

As covered in Chapter 3, the *vitis vinifera* grape has a high level of natural sugars within it. These sugars directly correlate to the alcohol levels in the wine. The fermentation process converts all the sugars to degrees of alcohol within the juice. If there are not enough sugars in the grape, the wine will have a very low-alcohol level and will be considered unstable. Often because of bad weather, poor soils, poor vine growing or mass production, the natural sugars in grapes are low. Therefore, the winemaker will add sugars to increase the alcohol levels and give the wine more weight.

Often smaller producers may have residual sugars leftover from the fermentation, when the climatic conditions that year have been more than favourable. These can be added back into the wine to create a seamless and more flavourful wine.

However, when we consider mass winemaking, the use of natural residual sugars to bump up their wines is just not a possibility – there simply wouldn't be the volume of reserves available. So processed sugars are added. Alongside processed sugars, additives, preservatives, colourings and a host of other manufactured ingredients are used.

For example, if you need very large quantities of wine by a certain date, you need to pick and include all of the grapes, no matter how ripe or rotten they are. You have a mandate to reach no matter the weather or the ripeness of the grapes.

If we take the case of Australian mass-scale winemaking, not all these grapes will be perfectly ripe, juicy and sugar-laden as required. Many are underripe, overripe, bland, too small, too big. It is virtually impossible to stand over the quality of each and every grape and ensure it has the correct ripeness levels required. So, it became a trend in the nineties to add sugar to the production of these wines to ensure volume levels were met despite weather conditions.

These are essentially factory-style wines: recipe wines that are created and crafted fully in the concrete buildings on the winery and not in the natural environment of the vineyards. Forecasted production levels need to be met no matter the weather or crop levels.

Here are some indicators of sugar levels in categories of wine. In your typical dry white or red wine, there should be less than 6 grams, and usually only 2 grams or less per litre.

- A Pinot Grigio from a small, quality-driven producer will have less than 2 grams of sugar per litre. On the contrary, a Pinot Grigio from a bigger producer could have over 12 grams of sugar per litre.
- A Malbec from a small producer based in Mendoza, Argentina, will have less than 5 grams of sugar, whereas mass-produced Malbec could have 14+ grams of sugar per litre.

- A Rioja Crianza from a smaller producer has less than 4 grams of sugar. A Crianza from a larger brand could have over 18 grams of sugar per litre.

Typical sugar content per 250ml glass of wine:

Sweet-white wine	235kcals 14.75g sugar
Medium-white wine	188kcals 7.5g sugar
Medium rosé	198kcals 6.25g sugar
Dry-white wine	188kcals 1.5g sugar
Red wine	190kcals 0.5g sugar

Technical wine classification for sugar levels:

Term	g/L residual sugar	calories of sugar
Bone dry	<1 g/L RS	0
Dry	1–10 g/L RS	0–6
Off-dry	10–35 g/L RS	6–21
Sweet	35–120 g/L RS	21–72
Very sweet	120–220 g/L RS	72–130

Generally speaking, red wines have the lowest amount of sugar at an average of less than 1-3 grams per litre. Dry white wines will average at 2-6 grams per litre, and rosé will average at 13-18 grams of sugar per litre.

Sadly, winemakers are not obliged to put the sugar

content on the label, so they don't! It is very tricky to gauge the sugar levels and as a result many of us are not aware of the sugar we are consuming in our wines. The only way to navigate your way around this is to try your best to choose wines from smaller, more quality-driven producers. Choosing these wines is something I will go into in extra detail in Chapter 6.

Other additives

We must remember that winemaking is an extremely unpredictable and volatile process. Millions of tiny micro-organisms are involved, due to the location of the grape growing in the fields, the presence of wild or commercial yeasts and the array of airborne smallies that fly through the winery at any given minute. This is a scientist's worst nightmare. Therefore the situation needs to be controlled, balanced and calmed by the use of additives. As mentioned, these are often harmless.

- **Acid blend** This is a mix of acids that help fermentation, flavour profiling and balancing the wine. The acids used are tartaric, citric and malic acid.
- **Commercial yeasts** These are added for predictability. Naturally produced yeast, which is found on the skins of the grapes, is unpredictable. It may work very well in one batch of wine, and then it'll be impossible to produce the same results twice. This is a non-negotiable for a big-brand wine that needs to taste the same year in, year out. You

may even have spoiled bacteria from the natural yeast in your fruit or flowers that is invisible, and this will destroy a batch of wine, making it undrinkable. Hence the popularity of cultured yeasts.

- **Finings** These are agents are used to help filter and fine the wine. They are generally gelatinous ingredients, such as isinglass, fish bones, animal proteins or egg whites. They draw the heavier particles down to the bottom of the tank, making it easier to remove them. With the growing rise in veganism, winemakers sometimes use bentonite clay as a vegan option to fine the wine.
- **Mega purple** This is used to bolster the colour of red wines. Particularly in mass winemaking, very often grapes are overcropped and bland. Naturally, the colour of the wine can seem lacklustre. In a visually obsessed world, we need the greenest apple, the bluest blueberries, the darkest chocolate. Foods and drinks are coloured. The same applies to mass-made wines. Wineries will use a mix called Mega Purple that is made from Rubired, a teinturier grape that is extremely rich in colour. 'Teinturier' is the French term for a grape with red skin and red flesh. To make this Mega Purple concoction, the grapes are prepared into a kind of sweet wine mix with a ton of residual sugar (about 68 per cent) and a very deep colour. Winemakers will also use Mega Purple to cover up the flavour of pyrazines, which are the compounds that give an unmistakable green bell-pepper flavour to certain wines made from Cabernet

Sauvignon. The high sugar levels can mask many an undesirable flavour in the wine. Mega Purple is often used, though generally in low doses. To be truthful, I have often looked at a wine and wondered is this the natural colour, as it looked so confected.

In theory it would be amazing to give you a bulletproof list of wineries that mass-scale produce, or an image of a wine label that clearly tells you if the wine is made by the millions or if the wine is from a zany winemaker who owns a tiny plot in the back of beyond. But sadly no such list exists. There is no magic wand to decipher a wine label as, truth be told, it is the one industry that still has the powers to elude on the label. There are very little governing laws that state the winery must display all their ingredients, let alone additives, allergens or even sugar levels. It seems crazy, but unfortunately this is true. We must navigate our way through the wine aisles with the sprinkling of knowledge you've learned here. Understand that wine is like any other product. If you see a wine that is sold in your local supermarket, in the petrol station, in a cinema, in a pub, in a quarter bottle at a festival, you must know that this is a beast that has probably been made in gargantuan proportions. On the other hand, if you are frequenting smaller local independent wine shops whose beating hearts are dedicated to wines, then this we must assume is the land of the smaller, better-quality wine producer. There are no hard and fast rules, apart from a lot of common sense and memory banking. Try to use wine apps like Vivino, Cellar Tracker or

Delectable. Also use your tasting skills once the wine is purchased. Test the length, test the fruit flavours, test the nose - are there many aromas or just one overriding aroma? And most importantly, take a note of the winery for wines you like, and look for them in future wine-buying escapades.

Chapter 5

What Grows Together, Goes Together: A Guide to Everyday Food and Wine Pairings

It's Christmas Day, circa 2010. I'm at the sink in our family home in Achill, washing the dishes for the millionth time. By this stage, I have somehow managed to pass my wine exams and, even bigger shock, I have landed a sommelier post in one of

Ireland's finest hotels. Sure, I'm like the 'queen of wine' in my family. God love them.

My brother, an extremely skilled chef, is making gravy by scalding the absolute bejaysus out of an oven tray that I will no doubt be washing. My sister, also a very accomplished chef, is shaking the pot of potatoes to make them super crispy for the boiling duck fat they will eventually go into. Another oven tray I will be washing. My other brother is roaming freely around the kitchen, awaiting his turn at washing the never-ending pile of dishes. He's a landscape gardener – and the poor guy has to listen to us drivel on about porcini mushrooms that pair so beautifully with a cheeky Dolcetto or a mineral-driven Sancerre that showcases a goat's cheese superbly. (Actually, that's a lie. I wouldn't be caught dead using a phrase like a 'cheeky Dolcetto', I'd probably used the term 'savage'. That's more my lingo.)

In any case, we'd spent hours spouting highfalutin nonsense and notions of finer things that we're normally not accustomed to. Acting like we ate and drank like this every day, when this wasn't the truth at all.

If I'm honest, the notion of food and wine pairing has gone daft altogether, with Michelin-star restaurants taking you on a food-and-wine-pairing journey that lasts about five hours, costs a small fortune and expands your waistline to that of an old-fashioned wrestler by the end of the meal. There's a fine line between recommending a red wine with your steak and recommending a Château Lynch-Bages with your mushroom duxelles, chateaubriand beef dish. For most of us mere mortals the latter scenario just ain't a thing. Our weekly repertoire of dishes is based more along the lines of spag bol, chicken stir-fry, ham and spuds, fish fingers and peas, and maybe even one of the evenings we'll go wild and have a spice bag delivered.

What the majority of us want to know is: If I have a glass of Sauv Blanc with my bag of M&Ms, will I be made a mockery of? Is a glass of Prosecco a valid choice for my Friday-night chicken burger? Will the men in white coats come to take me away if I have a glass of Cabernet Sauvignon whilst chomping down on my roast-chicken dinner on a Sunday afternoon?

While we might think that a quality bottle of wine will be a good match regardless, this is far from the real truth. Spending money does not absolutely guarantee the most favourable outcome. An expensive bottle of wine that tastes incredible on its own but is paired with a food that is turning it sour is a semi-disaster. Money down the drain. Here's a scenario: you made the extra journey to the independent wine store to try and get some advice on a good-quality bottle of wine to serve to your guests at dinner. The friendly wine nerd is chatting and chatting about the flavours and aromas and lord knows what else – but he forgets to ask you what you're eating. You wander off home with an oaked Chardonnay that cost you €25 under your arm. However, as you finally sit down to enjoy your own food, you can see bemused looks on your friends' faces. Your bestie is even going so far as a double eyebrow raise. You taste your lamb stew that has been stewing away for five hours. Soft like butter. You then taste your Chardonnay, and it doesn't quite taste right. But how? What's happened? The wine seems as if it has been watered down.

There are several factors to consider here.

The heat, the texture of the meat and the powerful flavours of the stew absolutely overpower the fruity notes in the Chardonnay. The very reason for stewing meats for hours in a sauce reduction is to intensify flavours. The pungent flavours and the sinew in the meat are way too big a match for even a medium-bodied Chardonnay. So, even though the wine won't do you any harm if you eat the wrong foods with it, the wine will taste sour or watery as the flavours vanish under a food that's far too powerful for it. And what is the point in spending your hard-earned cash on a wine experience that is watery and lacking in flavour?

Food and wine history

Before technology, travel and globalisation, people sat down to a meal and poured themselves a glass of wine that they had likely bought from a neighbour or made themselves. For the vast majority of wine's 6000-year history, people always drank wine made from grapes that were grown locally. Most wines were field blends (a variety of grapes grown altogether in one field), so people either drank a glass of 'red' or a glass of 'white'.

Our friends the Greeks and Romans began cultivating and producing grapes to suit certain local food styles. They knew all about the nutritional value of wine, and it became an inseparable part of their daily nourishment, often diluted with water to ensure it was consumed at every meal.

For the Romans, there are documented articles about the pairing of local eel with a decent 'Phalernum', a wine that is produced in Naples, and references to the wines of Friuli-Venezia Giulia pairing well with the local prosciutto.

This is probably one of your most basic and important things to consider when matching wine to a food – are they grown together? Are they from the same region climatically and culturally? This will automatically be a winner. For example, if I am drinking an Albariño from the northwestern coast of Spain, I will choose some fried white fish, as that is a dish of this region. If I am eating pizza, I will choose an Italian red that goes with tomatoes, like Chianti.

By the time of the Renaissance, food and wine pairing was flourishing. Recipe books were a common practice and these included suggested wines or beers to accompany certain dishes, revealing an early understanding of how certain flavours complemented each other.

By this time, the spice routes and various other trade partnerships were in full flow, and ingredients were an evolving commodity. As a result, recipes, cookbooks and culinary arts in general were thriving. There was far more of a concentration towards pairing your beverage with your food around this time. Wines had developed to be a far superior quality, and foods were fused through the colonial crusades to create local delicacies.

Fast forward to today and the dizzying heights of the culinary world and what all of us home cooks aspire to. Chefs are celebrities within themselves, sommeliers are growing in numbers every day, and they are studying chemical reactions within our mouths to create even more harmonious pairings. And, with the advances of social media and certainly since Covid, the interest in home dining has elevated to gastronomic proportions.

Today, it's less about sustenance and more about experimentation and creating memorable experiences with friends. Less about the preparation weeks in advance and serving it on fine bone china plates, and more about making it together and possibly sitting on the floor whilst others sit at the coffee table. The focus is on good food with amazing wines and even better company. This considered new art form is ensuring a symbiosis between the food and wine, and both components bringing out the best in each other.

In the past, food and wine pairing was far easier, as the food and wine were local to each other, as mentioned. To be fair to these gifted winemakers of the past, from Neolithic people to the Greeks and Romans, to those of the Middles Ages and so forth, options were limited in terms of culinary fusions. So, they worked with what they had.

However, the modern world is a far smaller place.

Today, shop shelves are filled with labels that include descriptions such as 'organic', 'biodynamic', 'oaked', 'unoaked', 'egg fermented', 'lees aged' and 'barrel fermented' - the list of wine-production techniques is endless, notwithstanding the number of grape varieties available. I empathise with the confusion levels you may feel.

In winemaking countries, they tend to stick to their own local grapes, and therefore their own local wines, to match their local foods. This makes for a far simpler and less confusing choice pattern. But, as we don't make our own classic wine styles here in Ireland, we have gargantuan levels of imports at our fingertips, as well as an array of cuisines to choose from. Most importantly, there are simply too many wines in the world with too many variations in cuisine style and ingredients, meaning absolutely no one can have an authority on every wine and food pairing. And I mean no one.

Having said that, there are some basic guidelines to food and wine pairing, especially when it comes to foods that we eat every day. Yeah, it's great learning about the pairing of lemon sole and Loire Valley Sauvignon Blanc or noisette of lamb with a Château Kirwan from Bordeaux. But honestly, who's eating lemon sole each week? Or starting their food-and-wine-pairing journey with an expensive Bordeaux? It is just not real life.

My aim is to help you discover an instinctive capability to match food and wine for yourself.

To do this, we need to think about how the primary food item is cooked. What is it served with? How is it flavoured? From supermarkets to epicurean food halls to online meal planners and countless takeaway offerings, our choice for weekly dinner options has never been more extensive, but before we completely overwhelm ourselves, let's concentrate on the basics.

When you are choosing the wine you are going to have with your meal, first consider the style of cooking.

- **Poaching and boiling** These are lighter styles of cooking that impart less flavours to the food, so they command a lighter wine, like a Beaujolais or a young Pinot Noir.
- **Roasting, BBQing and chargrilling** These are the most robust styles of cooking, and therefore impart plenty of flavours to the food, so they seek heavier wines like oaked Shiraz or an Argentinian Malbec.

The new trend of using air fryers imparts a degree of flavour, but is a far less intrusive style of cooking compared to roasting or BBQing.

Another consideration worth noting is the preparation of the foods. For example, a plain fillet of chicken placed straight on to a pan is very different from a fillet that has been left to marinate overnight in a tandoori-style yogurt dressing. Consider the spices that may have been added, or the seasoning and herbs that will greatly affect the flavours in foods.

If you have a piece of beef that has been rolled in creole spices and cooked in a pan, this will be far more fragrant than a piece of untouched beef that is cooked as is.

Similarly, the type of sauce you are serving is also an

incredibly vital part of the consideration for your wine. A pungent sauce, like curry, dominates the dish, and it is irrelevant whether you're using red or white meat – the essence of the dish lies in the sauce. Similarly, if you're serving a grilled steak, take note of the difference between pepper sauce, garlic butter or Béarnaise sauce. All have wildly different ingredients, therefore, the wine has to be chosen, not just based on the cut of meat, but also on the accompanying sauce.

Finally, there is a considerable difference between a sauce-based dish like curry, casserole, stew or stroganoff, and a piece of meat that may have a sauce as a garnish. So think about the impact of the sauce amount on the dish.

Perfect pairings

Same-same
Pair light-bodied wines with lighter dishes and full-bodied wines with heartier, more robust dishes.

Top tip
When deciding if the wine is light-bodied or full-bodied compare its texture to the weight of water (light body) or full-fat cream (full-bodied).

For example, pair a light Pinot Grigio with a piece of breaded fish, like a Donegal Catch. Yes, the coating will add a bit of weight to the fish but, ultimately, the fish is lightweight. Similarly, pair a rich and full-bodied Malbec or an oaked Chardonnay with a juicy homemade beef burger. The weight of the wine is strong enough to stand up against the fatty, rich burgers.

When talking about matching intensity, it is also important to consider matching the flavour intensities. For example, a Muscadet wine that has a light flavour intensity needs to be paired with foods that are lightly flavoured, such a white fish or poached chicken. For something intensely flavoured, like a Marlborough Sauvignon Blanc, you need to pair this with a marinated chicken breast or a pesto pasta bake. The likes of a Muscadet or Pinot Grigio would be lost under the pungency of the herb pesto or spicy marinade. All the flavours would be killed off.

Looking into acidity, tannins and bubbles

Acidity

Aim to balance the acidity levels in the food and the wine.

High-acid wines (which are recognisable through their mouth-watering effect), like Sauvignon Blanc, suit foods with high acidity, like a tangy creamy cheese or a tomato-based focaccia. Elevated levels of acidity can cut through the richness of creamy dishes, as well as fatty, greasy foods. Because acidity stimulates your saliva glands, this makes your mouth water. The extra saliva simply cleanses your tongue after each bite. Genius really. The high levels of acidity are also helpful in keeping your palate fresh and preventing tasting fatigue.

Think of high-acid wines for the likes of those mammoth dining meals like Christmas Day. The acidity keeps your palate alive after the onslaught of five million ingredients.

Pairing
- Pinot Noir with Christmas Day lunch
- Chianti with spaghetti bolognese
- Sauvignon Blanc with creamy goat's cheese

Tannins

These are the components of wine – they are found in the skins of grapes – that literally dry out your gums. They're an antioxidant and also a preservative. Winemakers may choose to leave the grapes on the skins for longer to achieve higher tannin levels if they want their wine to age longer. Hence the preservative affect. However, when a wine has high levels of tannins, it can feel very drying and sometimes unpleasant.

To combat tannins, choose a food with high levels of protein. Generally, certain grapes are known to have higher tannins because they have thicker skins, e.g. Cabernet Sauvignon, Shiraz, Nebbiolo, Tannat and Tempranillo. Proteins in foods are able to melt away the tannins – literally. Please believe me when I say there is a massive difference between tasting a tannic red on its own and tasting a tannic red with some hard vintage cheddar or some sinewy meat, like a ribeye steak. You could almost mistake the wine as two different wines. Moral of the story is - if you open your wine and you're shocked by the tannin level, reach for a piece of hard cheese like Cheddar, Parmesan or Manchego, and don't panic.

This is a desirable quality in wine that winemakers use to cut through rich foods, but also to freshen your mouth by drying it out.

Pairing
- Any vintage cheddar with French Cabernet Sauvignon
- Nebbiolo with grilled ribeye steak
- Shiraz with lamb cutlets

Bubbles

Sparkling wines - Champagne, Prosecco, Cava or Crémant - are super versatile. Some clever marketing genius way back when convinced us that wines with bubbles in them are only for celebrating with, so these are generally consumed without foods. However, the bubbles make them some of the most food-friendly wines there are.

In Chapter 7, I'll talk about how sparkling wines are made and how incredibly popular they are in today's world but, for now, I just want to concentrate on their ability to lift a dining experience.

To keep the bubbles fresh, there is usually exceptionally high acidity. These naturally made bubbles are in their millions within one bottle, and the acidity will easily cut through rich, greasy foods. The very nature of the bubbles is lightweight, refreshing and a marvel for cleansing your tongue for the next bite, much like the properties of acidity.

Dangerously enough, this style of wine keeps your palate so fresh throughout this experience, it leads you to thinking you can reach for more, even after you've finished your own portion.

Most Michelin-starred restaurants that have a seven- or nine-course tasting menu will have at least two sparkling wines to pair with the courses. Generally, these will be quality-made Champagne, one white and one rosé. Their effervescence and acidity make them suitable for salty, fried or spicy foods. So, remember next time you open your bottle of bubbles, don't be afraid to whip out a bit of hummus or cured meats to pair with it.

Pairing
- Fish and chips from your favourite local chipper with Crémant de Loire
- Prosecco with Parma harm
- Champagne with smoked salmon

Flavour or not to flavour – complement or contrast

Scientists describe seven basic tastes: bitter, salty, sour, astringent, sweet, pungent (e.g. chilli) and umami. As mentioned previously, there are five basic tastes that the tongue is sensitive to: salt, sweet, bitter, sour and umami.

There can also be physical changes within the mouth – such as a coating of fat or thick sticky textures or hot impressions from temperatures, like alcohol or spices.

And, just to add even more confusion, humans can detect 10,000 or so aromas. These aromas reach the taste receptors through the nose and travel through the nasal passage that connects with the mouth. So, as you chew your food, 'smellable' vapours increase, and the perception of taste can change as these additional aromas are registered.

In layman's terms, aromas that travel up your nose can affect the taste of the food you eat.

No one wants to eat their food in a smelly bathroom or beside someone who is drenched in an overpowering cologne. It is retch-worthy. We are sensitive souls and the most sensitive parts of our bodies are not our broken hearts but our tasting sensations – and they can be easily swayed.

When we are considering flavours, it is key to ask if our wine is clashing with our food. Are we inhaling pungent curry aromas whilst trying to sip a light-flavoured Muscadet? Or are we inhaling vibrant tropical fruits found in New Zealand Sauvignon Blanc and missing the delicate flavours of clams or mussels?

Instead, look for **complementary** flavours between the food and the wine.

Pairing
- Mushrooms with an earthy Pinot Noir
- Citrusy Sauvignon Blanc with a white fish in a lemon sauce
- Super-fruity, rich Australian Shiraz with a BBQed beef-burger

Contrasting flavours can also create excellent pairings. Think of peanut butter and jam, possibly one of the most popular sandwiches, and one that my kids love. Personally, I find it gross but I can understand the dynamic.

What I do love is salted caramel. I am an absolute sucker for the pink-Himalayan salted caramel Butlers Chocolate. When that sweet and savoury combination is delicately handled, magic happens. (And I like to enjoy this chocolate with Primitivo, a southern Italian red.)

Pairing
- Riesling with smoked-bacon salad
- Blue cheese with a port
- Prosecco with popcorn

Mind the sweetness – real versus fake

Since human tastebuds are more susceptible to acidity and bitterness than sweetness, you may be blissfully unaware of the amount of sugar used in making wine. Today's foods are filled with processed ingredients and processed sugars but, truthfully, without sugar we would have no wine.

The natural sugars in grapes are converted to alcohol through fermentation, making this the crucial aspect that differentiates a simple grape juice from wine. But when pairing wine and food, it's important to think about the difference between natural sugars and fake sugars. There are vast differences between the two. Remember my analogy on p.55 of comparing real fruit flavours and aromas to fake-fruit aromas and flavours like those found in Starburst or Chewits sweets.

Top tip

If the flavour of your wine seems strange, always think about what you've just eaten. Foods like aubergine, asparagus, mints, peanut butter, mayonnaise, ice cream, vinegar and spines like cloves, saffron and nutmeg can play havoc with the delicate flavours of wine.

See Chapter 4 for a discussion of the perils of mass winemaking and sloppy use of added sugars in many of the well-known brands that line our shop shelves.

As explained in Chapter 3, the *vitis vinifera* grape has a high level of natural sugars within it. These sugars directly correlate to the alcohol levels in the wine. The fermentation process converts all the sugars to degrees of alcohol within the juice. If there are not enough sugars in the grape, the wine will have a very low alcohol level and will be considered unstable. Often due to bad weather, poor soils, poor vine growing or mass production the natural sugars in the grapes are low. As we know the winemaker will add sugars to bump up the alcohol levels and give the wine more weight. And this is more common practice among big winemakers who produce on a large scale.

My biggest tip for a wine with elevated sugar levels is to pair these wines with salty or spicy foods like Asian fusion style cuisine. For example, pairing a sweet wine like a Riesling with a spicy curry will balance the heat of the food.

Top wine pairings with everyday foods

The very essence of this book is to enjoy wine without all the snobbery and the fuss. Too often I see wine and food pairings with foods us mere mortals may only make once a year. The white tablecloth is dusted down, the heat is lashed on in the empty, cold, rarely used dining room. The granny blinds are drawn in to serve a random risk of a dinner like beef Wellington or a lobster thermidor. In my house we couldn't be further from this. I like a mid-week glass of wine with something that won't take a bevy of half-qualified chefs to make. Chances are I am eating one of the following dishes. So here is what I would pair with them.

- **Spaghetti bolognese** Red wines with high acidity and tannins – Chianti, Nero d'Avola. For white, pair it with Verdicchio from Tuscany.
- **Thai green curry** Off-dry wines like a Pinot Gris from New Zealand or Alsace. Be brave and try a German Riesling from the Mosel Valley – you'll be delighted you did.
- **Irish stew** A soft, rich full-bodied red like a well-made Argentinian Malbec or a French Côtes du Rhône.
- **Shepherd's pie** An acidic, fruity red like a Côtes du Rhône or a New Zealand Pinot Noir. An oaked Chardonnay would also work here if you fancy a white wine.
- **Lasagne** A selection of Italian reds like a Chianti, Barbera, Dolcetto or else a Sicilian Nero D'Avola.
- **Donegal Catch haddock** Pairs well with a fruity Albariño or else a French Loire Valley Sauvignon Blanc like a Touraine.
- **Chilli con carne** A sweet red-berry, fruity red like a Spanish Garnacha from Navarra or Penedès, or head to the south of Italy for a Primitivo. The sweetness of the ripe berries will soothe the spice of the chilli.
- **Chicken fajitas** Always go well with an oaked Chardonnay from Mâcon-Villages. Or try a really warm and ripe Vermentino from Sardinia.
- **Chicken curry from the takeaway** A wine with a touch of extra sweetness to pair with the strong spices. Choose a decent off-dry Riesling from Australia or Germany. If you prefer to go for a red, go wild and try a red-ale beer. Red wines will just turn metallic under the pungency of the spices.

- **Spicebag** Wine that's light, refreshing and palate cleansing – the ideal wine would be a glass of Prosecco, Cava or Champagne. Most reds will be destroyed by this food.
- **Ham and cheese toastie** Lighter reds with high acidity. Think Beaujolais, like a Fleurie or a Morgon, or a German Pinot Noir. The high acidity glides through the melted cheese.
- **Roast chicken with all the trimmings** White with weight and power, like a fruity Chardonnay or else a Bordeaux Blanc. The added oak ageing gives the wine more weight to cope with all the flavours.
- **Irish fry** Wine with plenty of acidity and some bubbles to thoroughly cleanse the palate after all the grease. The sweet peach and apricot flavours of a Prosecco Spumante will contrast nicely with all the saltiness of this dish.
- **Tayto cheese and onion crisps** Soft, fruity white like a French Viognier or an Italian Lugana. But, to be fair to these iconic crisps, I've often had them in the pub with a glass of Sauvignon Blanc and they've worked a charm.
- **Bag of Manhattan popcorn (or any popcorn really)** A super-fruity glass of Prosecco or maybe a Crémant d'Alsace.
- **Super Noodles** A light, fruity white or red wine that will not overpower the lightness of the noodles. This is very subjective, though – I like to add soy sauce, coriander and sesame seeds to mine.
- **Hummus and crackers** A hearty wine, like the earthy flavours in a Languedoc red like Minervois, will work well

here. These are generally soft and juicy reds, with a touch of local Mediterranean herbs.

- **Tacos** Think about the meat here. If it's chicken use a lighter red with plenty of fruit flavours, like an Italian Valpolicella. If it's beef use a Spanish Rioja that has been oak-aged. The oak ageing will give the wine a bit more weight to stand up to the robust red meat and collection of spices.

- **Bacon and cabbage** An Irish classic that deserves a wine with generous natural sugar levels to contrast with the salty ham. Think of a white from Alsace like a Pinot Blanc or an off-dry Riesling. (Please don't be scared of Rieslings, they are so good!)

- **Slow-cooker chicken casserole** A full wine that is bursting with intense flavours. Think of a well-made buttery Chardonnay, like Mâcon-Villages, or an oaked red, like a Ribera del Duero from Spain.

- **Chicken noodle soup** The delicate flavours and light weight of the soup need a wine that won't spoil that. Try a light and crisp Muscadet or a Loire Valley Sauvignon Blanc.

- **Tomato soup** A sweet red with a luscious weight is required to combat the pungency and acidity in tomatoes (though rendering them down into a soup will remove a lot of it). Try a Valpolicella or a Barbera.

- **Ice cream** Wine that is rich, sweet and palate coating to counter the sweetness and numb tastebuds. Try the famous dark sherry from Spain called Pedro Ximénez. For one better, pour the dark sherry over the ice cream and slip away into a food and wine utopia.

- **Milk chocolate** If you're chomping down on a square of Dairy Milk, you could pair this with a Sauternes. This is a sweet-honeyed wine made in Bordeaux that has flavours of tangerines, rhubarb and honey. There is just enough sweetness and weight in this wine to pair with chocolate.

- **Grilled white fish** Red wines such as a young Pinot Noir or a Beaujolais or even an Italian Valpolicella.

- **Oily fish (sardines, salmon or some anchovies)** A Pinot Noir would work if you wanted a red wine, but a dry, acidic white from Bordeaux made from Sauvignon Blanc would work a charm here.

- **Eggs** Bubbles seem to lighten the richness of an omelette. This is a nod to the sweet and savoury here, so pairing your eggs with a light and fruity Prosecco would work well.

- **Pasta pesto** Complement the basil with a fresh and herbaceous white wine. Check out a grassy Sauvignon Blanc from the Loire Valley or a Grüner Veltliner from Austria.

- **Chicken goujons** A French Chardonnay from the Mâcon region is a great option here. There's plenty of sunshine there in the summer, so flavours are ripe and fruity, making this a happy pairing alongside the nutty crust on the chicken pieces.

Styles of wine ranging from lightest to fullest:

- **Sparkling wine** Prosecco, Asti Spumante, Crémant, Cava, Champagne
- **Dry white wine** Touraine Sauvignon Blanc, Veneto Pinot Grigio, Rueda Verdejo
- **Sweet white wine** Sauternes Bordeaux, Hungarian Tokaji, French Muscat Beaume de Venise
- **Rich white wine** Oaked French Chardonnay, Rhône Valley Viognier, White Rioja
- **Rosé wine** Provence Rosé, Tuscan Rosé, Navarra Rosé
- **Light red wine** Beaujolais, Italian Dolcetto, Austrian Zweigelt
- **Medium red wine** Loire Valley Cabernet Franc, Spanish Mencia, Italian Chianti
- **Bold red wine** Italian Amarone, Rhône Valley Châteauneuf-du-Pape, Argentinian Malbec
- **Dessert wine** Tuscan Vin Santo, Spanish Pedro Ximenez, Dark Australian Muscat

Chapter 6

Pour-fection Selection: Matching Wines to Elevate Your Dinner Party

> *Did you know?*
> *The world's largest wine bottle is called*
> *Maximus, and it was crafted by Swiss engineers.*
> *With a colossal 13cm-thick glass and standing*
> *over 4 feet tall, this extraordinary bottle holds*
> *an impressive 490 litres of wine, equivalent*
> *to a staggering 654 regular-sized bottles.*

I read in an article recently that the notion of the dinner party is now dead. And it made me think. In fairness, it's been a while since I've been invited to a proper dinner party. You know like those big dinner parties that have a cross-section of humanity at the table and it is as tense as a gripping episode of *Mastermind*. At the table would be a heady mix of a 'freegan' tofu lover, a foreign-politics obsessive, a pair of IFSC ex-'Rock boys, a couple of GAA hurlers, some outrageously glamorous TikTok influencers and a random Gen Xer looking to play Def Leppard. Can you imagine the craic? To me that sounds like a nightmare. Albeit I'm Gen X also, I would be inclined to sway with the millennials and consider the idea of a dinner party fairly antiquated.

Put it this way, myself, my sister and my cousins did *Come Dine With Me* for years. We still try, to be fair, but we have had countless children, work promotions, books, PhDs and lord knows whatever else to keep us busy. Nonetheless, when the opportunity arises we rock up to the designated host's house. We deck ourselves in the fancy-dress theme of the evening. If the cuisine was French, we adorned ourselves in baguettes and nautical T-shirts. When the theme was Indian, we went full Bollywood glamour. The last one we had was a Spanish theme. All the girls were dolled up to the nines in their flamenco dresses and matador outfits, but I for some reason came as Enrique Iglesias. I bought a cardboard cutout of his face and wore the mask. I acquired a boy's black wig and bought a T-shirt that had a fake six pack on it. It looked like I was in the nude from the jeans up. I borrowed my friend's jeans and wore his size 10 trainers. I looked a state – but a funny state.

I would never be one to assume that no one is having formal dinner parties in their houses any more. I'm sure there are plenty out there that enjoy hosting friends over a large table with good food, good wine and good conversation flowing. So, what I will do with this chapter is go through the courses that generally exist in dinner parties and suggest some styles of wines that would suit each course.

As there are countless recipes out there, and even more wine styles still, I'll stick to general guidelines.

Dinner party dos and don'ts

Top tip
Open and taste your wines long before your guests arrive. This will save you the heartache of possibly serving a corked wine.

Before you start choosing your wines, bear the following in mind.

- The wines should always go up in terms of weight, alcohol and flavour intensity. This means you are starting off with low-alcohol white or sparkling wines, then move up to lighter whites or reds, then medium- to full-bodied whites or reds, then finally you finish with high-alcohol, rich wines to cut through the sweetness in the dessert. These are general rules you should try and stick by. Yes, of course, Uncle Mike can have his powerhouse Aussie Shiraz to start as he walks in the door. But if you serve this style of wine to everyone in the room, they would be suitably jarred by the time the starter arrived and their tastebuds would be obliterated by the alcohol, robust dark fruits and gripping tannins. Light to full is always the best way to go.

- Serve water generously throughout the evening. We all have different tipping points when it comes to alcohol, and as the host it is down to us to keep a mindful eye on who's consuming what and how they're enjoying themselves. Food has a great part to play in soaking up the alcohol; however, many of us won't be aware of the alcohol levels in the wine. We are drinking in a subconscious manner, so we are sipping and chatting. We are less likely to look at the back of the bottle because we are socialising and relaxing. It is up to the host to manage this. Water, sparkling or still, is an ally in terms of managing your guests and their alcohol intake.

- Pour small servings of wine into the glass. Yes, this will make more work for you, however the wine needs room in the glass to breathe. I generally try to use wine glasses that have a decent base and funnel in at the top. This way the aromas are travelling to the nose while you sip, and this is, of course, improving the flavour intensity of the wine. This type of glass also enables a good swirl, which is so important to open the wine up before each sip.

- Serve your wines at the right temperature. This is so important, as it will change the flavour of the wine to something unfamiliar if not. Styles of wine are produced with serving temperatures in mind. If you serve a white wine that's too warm the acids go down and the fruits go up. All of a sudden, you're drinking a white wine that feels flabby and weighty, and the fruit flavours feel way more pronounced. On the other side, if you serve a red wine too chilled, the acids will go up and the fruit flavours will dimmish slightly and it becomes a far more austere red than you chose in the shop.

Temperatures for serving

Wine	Type	Temperature (°C)
Vintage port	Fortified wine	19°C
Bordeaux, Shiraz	Red wine	18°C
Red Burgundy, Cabernet	Red wine	17°C
Rioja, Pinot Noir	Red wine	16°C
Chianti, Zinfandel	Red wine	15°C
Tawny/NV port	Fortified wine	14°C
Beaujolais, rosé	White wine/rosé	12°C
Viognier, Sauternes	White wine	11°C
Chardonnay	White wine	9°C
Riesling	White wine	8°C
Champagne, sparkling wine, dessert wine	Sparkling wine/dessert wine	7°C
Ice wines	Dessert wine	6°C
Asti Spumante	Sparkling wine	5°C

- Taste your red wines a couple of hours before you serve them. They may possibly need an hour or two in a decanter. Now, when I say decanter, this can mean any vessel that you can pour wine into. This may be a large bowl, a large cup, a jug – anything really that can hold the liquid. The most important thing is the air rushing into the liquid as it leaves the bottle. If you are in a super hurry, transfer the wine from the bottle to the jug a number of times quite quickly. The most important thing is getting oxygen into the wine rapidly. The flip side of this is that you shouldn't leave your wine too long in a decanter. Over-airing it will start to kill all the fruit flavours.

So how do you know a wine needs to be decanted?

When you first open your bottle of red, and if you feel the aromas are very dull and lacklustre, the wine could most likely do with a decant, especially if you have spent a little bit of money on the bottle. Very often the producer will make the wine to age – so it is suitable to drink in ten years' time. When we are drinking these wines, they are too young, and we need to find a way to speed up the ageing process.

As wines age in a barrel, they enjoy a reaction to the minimal contact with oxygen over time through the pores in the wood. By pouring the wine out of the bottle and into another vessel the wine is absorbing oxygen. When it lies in a decanter the circumference of the liquid will receive the air, so it's important to swirl the decanter also to help the airing process. Test the wine after an hour and see if the fruits are more vibrant.

If it is still muted, leave it and check again in another half hour. But remember not to leave your wine too long in the decanter as the excess of oxygen will kill off the fruit aromas. Check the wine every half hour.

You can decant white wines and leave the decanter in the fridge. Decanting white wines is usually reserved for higher quality wines that have been aged under oak for a couple of years. The majority of white wines are made to drink straightaway (within one to two years after production).

- To speed chill your white or sparkling wines, wet a piece of kitchen paper. Wrap it around the wine bottle and pop in your freezer and your wine will be chilled in around fifteen minutes. Sparkling wines especially need to be served very chilled.

- If you need to keep your wine on ice all evening, add a little water and salt to the ice and this will keep the wine at a cold temperature. The salt will lower the freezing point, leaving the ice to melt slower over the course of the evening.

Canapés and finger foods

Canapés are tiny little servings of your choice. Theoretically, they should be one-bite sized. The actual meaning of a canapé is a piece of sliced bread with a topping, but, at this stage, we take it to mean any tiny little piece of finger food.

It doesn't really matter what you call them, the theory behind these little nibbles is to offer your guests a taste of what is to come. Truth be told, most wines are made with food in mind. Most wines are not made for me and my pals watching Netflix and skulling wine with no food or no thought. So at this stage of the evening, you're offering your guests something to taste while they sip down a cold glass of crisp wine.

Whether you're eating a cured salmon crudité or a mackerel blini or maybe something a little more old school like pineapple and cheese, the weight of the food item is important here. It is light. So, your wines will be light. A major component to an opening wine is also to whet the appetite. To get the juices flowing. What's ideal for this is a light and refreshing wine that is high in acidity and will literally make your mouth water.

We use champagne-style glasses for these types of wines. They have a narrow bowl and opening that directs all the delicate flavours of your opening wine to your nose. These glasses enhance lighter wines that are often the wine you begin your evening with.

Champagne glass

A good place to start for these wines is cool-climate countries, where there are generally fewer sunshine hours, therefore less ripeness in the grapes and higher levels of acidity. Think of northern France, Germany, England, Tasmania in Australia and Oregon in the US, especially grapes like Chardonnay and Sauvignon Blanc.

Another benefit to choosing a white with high acidity is the ability of the acids to cut through rich foods. In general, white wines are produced in a lighter style than reds due to less skin contact and no use of skins or seeds during fermentation. This enables a far lighter juice with a clear colour and is in line with popular demand for white wine.

On the next page is a table of common canapés and the wines that pair well with them.

Raw fish	Unoaked French Chardonnay (high acidity, zesty appeal, generous citrus fruits complement the soft flavours of raw fish)
Smoked fish	Muscadet Sur Lie (bone dry, high acidity, light crisp weight, cuts right through oily fish)
Salted nuts	Albariño (bursting with tropical fruits, high acidity, saline element that combats the saltiness of the nuts)
Oysters	Good-quality Champagne/Crémant (high acidity, light weight, plenty of bubbles to cleanse the palate after a salty oyster)
Liver pâté	Oloroso sherry (bone dry, nutty flavours, warm alcohol that cuts right through the richness of the pâté)
Mushroom vol au vent	German Riesling (dry, light weight, incredible acidity levels, ripe fruits and honey tones that will contrast with the earthy mushroom)
Pineapple and cheese	Prosecco or Spumante (dry, light weight, gentle bubbles and flavours of apricot and peach that will complement the salty cheese)
Beef carpaccio	Dolcetto Italian red (dry, soft mouthfeel, bright cherry flavours that contrast with the earthy beef tones. Beautiful acidity that cleanses the palate also)
Potato croquettes	Cava (high acidity, plenty of bubble to cleanse the palate, green apples and lime skin to contrast with the creamy potato)

And here is a table of wines that are suitable for most canapés.

Sparkling	• Crémant de Loire, Crémant de Bourgogne and Crémant d'Alsace – Caves de Lugny • Prosecco Spumante – Rizzardi, Veneto • Good-quality Cava – Perelada, Catalunya
White wines	• Muscadet – Jeremy Huchet • Albariño – Terras Gauda, Picpoul de Pinet – Domaine de Sol • German Riesling – Geil, Unoaked Chardonnay – Domaine Brocard Chablis • Gavi di Gavi – Picollo Ernesto, Loire Chenin Blanc – Les Caves de la Loire

Rosé wines	• Provence rosé – Château Minuty • German rosé – Thorle Rheinhessen • Loire Valley rosé – Marquis de Golaine, Rosé d'Anjou
Red wines	• Dolcetto – Cascina Carlot 'San Rumu', German Pinot Noir – Becker Family Pfalz • Beaujolais – Domaine Jean Folliard, Bardolino – Zenato

Starters

The meaning of the word 'appetiser' is a food or drink that stimulates the appetite before the main meal. Effectively these foods occupy the mind while we wait for the main masterpiece that will fill our bellies.

One of the first documentations of the word is in the third century BCE, when the Greeks were creating charcuterie-style boards with a mish-mash of foods to begin proceedings at their long, illustrious banquets. Both the Greeks and the Romans are often depicted visually in art enjoying fruit, nuts and meats before a large meal. This course also lengthens the dining experience without filling people up too much.

The starters, no matter the ingredients, will be richer and weightier than the canapés, therefore the wines must match. There are, of course, crossovers, as many of the lighter wines have powerful acidity that is a great palate cleanser after rich, succulent ingredients. But, in general, the servings are small so a big wine might overshadow the delicacy of the starter.

For these wines, we use a white wine glass. Here the bowl

of the glass is typically wider to allow a fuller expression of a wine and more room to swirl and breathe. There is still a narrower opening to direct all the aromas to your nose.

White wine glass

Below is a table of common starters and the wines that pair well with them.

Smoked salmon	Crémant rosé (the extra skin contact gives a little more weight, and a little more red-berry flavours to contrast with the oily salmon)
Prawn cocktail	Picpoul de Pinet (these seaside vineyards give grapes that benefit from both the Mediterranean sun and sea. The ripe fruits will partner the prawns perfectly)
Goat's/feta cheese	Sauvignon Blanc (the high acidity cleans the palate after the creamy cheese)
Ceviche	Grüner Veltliner (high acidity and gorgeous green-apple fruit will complement the tangy soft fish)
Parma ham with peach slices	Prosecco or Cava (the peach flavours will highlight the peach slices and contrast with the salty ham)

Below is a table of wines that are suitable for most starters.

Sparkling wines	• Prosecco Spumante Valdobbiadene DOCG – Santa Margarita, Champagne AOP – Pannier • Crémant de Loire Rosé AOP – Château Langlois Loire Valley (Bollinger owned) • Cava DO – Peres Balta Brut Vintage
White wines	• Loire Valley Chenin Blanc AOP – Saumur Château de Villeneuve, Albariño DO – Mar de Frades • Vermentino DOC – Trulli, Godello Valdeorras DO – Gargola Godello • Lugana DOC – Sirmione, Alsace Riesling AOP – Meyer Fonne
Red wines	• Pinot Noir NZ Bierzo Mencia AOP • Fleurie AOP • Huia Pinot Noir NZ • Bodeags Valdesil Bierzo Mencia DO • Joseph Drouhin Fleurie AOP

Soup

At this stage, your guests are craving a lighter feel to the meal. Whether you're serving a broth that has meat in it, a clear soup or a hearty starch-fuelled soup, the wines will all mirror the weight of the starter wines.

The more important thing here is the main ingredients of the soup, which will dictate the flavours of wine. All soups have roughly the same weight and are usually served in a smaller measure than normal. It is a handy way to lengthen a meal and to highlight the skills of the cook. We need to consider the thickness, temperature and mouthfeel of the soup when choosing an ideal wine.

For certain soups, red wine may be best suited. Red wine glasses have a far larger bowl then white glasses. This is to allow a far greater degree of oxygen to swirl around the glass with the weightier wine. Very often tannins will need to be softened and this is best achieved in a wider glass like this.

Red wine glass

Below is a table of common soups and the wines that pair well with them.

Gazpacho	Oloroso DO (this dry nutty sherry is high in acidity to match the cold tomatoes, and the nutty aromas will contrast with the sweet, ripened tomatoes)
Minestrone	Barbera DOC (this is an earthy, fruity light weight red that will harmonise with this light broth-style soup)
Tom Yum Gai	Off-dry Alsace Riesling DOP (if you have a little spice in your soup, like this hot and sour Thai soup, a touch of sweetness is always good with chilli)

Homemade vegetable soup	Mâcon-Village Chardonnay AOP (for an earthy, yet sweet flavoured soup, a Chardonnay with just a lick of oak will have plenty of fruit characters to combat the weight)

Main course

This is, of course, the star of the evening. The crescendo of the culinary workings. It is always advisable to leave a long enough gap between the starter and the main course so diners can work up an appetite again.

At this stage, wines are changed over; water is topped up and maybe a bit of music is played to add a layer of entertainment. Depending on how formal your dinner is, it's usually advisable to change to bigger glass for this course. Generally, the wines served with the main course are a little more serious and, therefore, deserve a large bowl for lots of swirling to open the wine up. Remember to pour a little in all the glasses at first to enable the wine to breathe properly. Richer dishes seek a rich, full-bodied wine that needs plenty of room to breathe and move around in the glass. The wider opening of the glass also allows for the intense and often alcohol-laden vapours to dissipate naturally while the glass is resting.

It would be impossible to list all the possible main-course ideas in the world, so I have taken the liberty of choosing what I think are the most popular types of dish. Always take into consideration the garnishes, sauces and gravies that are served with your main course and remember to initially pair your wine with your foods in theory, but also test them together long before the big day.

When it comes to meats, note of the major differences in the flavours between the cooking styles – roasting versus poaching or chargrilling versus steaming. The heavier the charring or roasting, the weightier the wine needs to be, and so forth.

Large red wine glass

Because of the many cooking methods, ingredients, sauces and side dishes, I have suggested wine pairings for the six most popular meats.

Beef	Cabernet Sauvignon, Grenache, Rioja Reserva, Shiraz, Nebbiolo and Malbec
Lamb	French Pinot Noir, Ribera del Duero, Bordeaux Blend, Merlot, Northern Rhône Syrah and Brunello di Montalcino
Chicken	Mâcon-Villages, Godello Valdeorras, Austrian Grüner Veltliner, Soave, Bordeaux Blanc and German Pinot Blanc

Pork	German Riesling, New Zealand Pinot Noir, Alsace Pinot Gris, Dolcetto, Beaujolais and Pouilly-Fuissé
Duck	French Pinot Noir, Burgundy oaked Chardonnay, Chianti, Nero d'Avola, Austrian Zweigelt and French Malbec
Turkey	Pouilly-Fuissé, Alsace Pinot Gris, New Zealand Sauvignon Blanc, Alsace Pinot Noir, Valpolicella and Barbera

For the most part, vegetarian dishes will have a lighter feel to them, in contrast to meaty style dishes. Often cheese, tomatoes, pumpkin, or aubergine will play a leading role. But vegetarian cooking is usually less about the main star, and more about the sum of all parts. So it's best to choose a wine that can match with several different ingredients well.

I have chosen five of the most popular vegetarian dishes here:

Mushroom risotto	German Pinot Noir, Fleurie, Spanish Garnacha, Mâcon Villages, Alsace Pinot Gris, or Champagne NV
Vegetarian lasagne	Chianti, Primitivo, Bordeaux AC, Nero d'Avola, or Vermentino, Godello for whites
Pumpkin soup	Albariño, Godello, off-dry German Riesling, Alsace Pinot Blanc, or a Languedoc Viognier
Aubergine Moussaka	Fruity Negroamaro, Aglianico, US Zinfandel, Lebanese Cabernet Sauvignon, or Côtes du Rhône Villages Rouge
Cauliflower steak	Chablis, Vouvray Chenin Blanc, Touraine Sauvignon Blanc, Soave, or Gavi di Gavi

When it comes to fish, there are a whole host of different types. Everything from soft white flaky fish like cod, to meaty textured fish like halibut, to sweet succulent shellfish like crab or lobster. Each texture deserves a wine of their own.

Soft, white fish (seabass, cod, haddock, etc.)	Albariño, Vinho Verde, Muscadet, French Sauvignon Blanc, Grüner Veltliner, or Bordeaux Blanc
Meaty fish (halibut, tuna, swordfish, etc.)	Crémant de Loire, Pouilly-Fuissé, Bordeaux Blanc, Gavi or Languedoc Viognier
Shellfish (crab, lobster, oysters, etc.)	Shellfish (crab, lobster, oysters, etc.) – Muscadet Sur Lie, Champagne, English Sparkling wine, German Riesling, Chablis, or Sancerre

Desserts

My dad always tells us he gets a headache after his dinner if he doesn't have a little sweet something, even if it is just a digestive biscuit. It soothes his cravings. Might I add, my father is eighty and still going strong – he's amazing.

Today, the mainstream media will have you frightened to even touch a piece of chocolate after your dinner because it will destroy your health. OK, I may be exaggerating, but lately sugar has a bad rep. My theory is everything in moderation. We are obviously not scoffing chocolate puddings seven days a week but, every now and then, it is one of life's pleasures to go the whole hog and indulge in a sickly sweet dessert.

We also often crave a little sugar after the main meal to balance out our palates, plus you get a little necessary pick-me-up from the sugar rush. Back in yesteryear or so, the Greeks and the Romans snacked on fruits or nuts with honey. Today, we are living it large in the world of chocolate fondant, strawberry pavlovas, Key lime pie or even a knickerbocker glory.

Dessert wine glass

Heaven knows the last thing we may want is a sweet wine to pair alongside the dessert. But hear me out.

There are many who will not have room for a dessert, and this is where a sweet wine will happily fill the sweet void. Your cravings are being satisfied without overloading on more food. The second reason why these wines are absolutely stunning is they have the magical ability to cleanse your palate after an attack of palate-clinging sugars.

For sweet wines after the main course, we use a small dessert wine glass, as the quantities drank here tend to be less than the wine we have drank with the meal up to now.

I will base the wines chosen on the sugar levels of the desserts. Naturally, a chocolate dessert will have a greater degree of sweetness in contrast to a lemon tart, which has an element of tart citrus flavours. The table on the following page provides pairings for different types of desserts.

Semi-sweet desserts (fruit-based tarts)	German Auslese Riesling (these incredible wines are honeyed and filled with tropical fruits, but have a tart, tangy, clean finish) – Thorle Riesling
Sweet desserts (pannacotta, crème brûlée or sponge cakes)	Sauternes (this Bordeaux sweet wine is like liquid tangerine and honey – it's smooth, yet finishes fresh to cleanse the palate) – Château Coutet, Bordeaux
Unctuously sweet desserts (chocolate fondant, crème caramel or ice cream)	Pedro Ximenez Sherry (this dark, super-sweet wine is like treacle; it is one of the few wines that has the capacity to pair with ice cream or milky chocolate and is often served over ice cream as a dessert in itself – it is incredible, please try it) – Lustao San Emilio

Cheeseboards

Cheese used to be served by itself with no bread or crackers. Today, these boards resemble a grazing board that factors in most of the food groups. They've become huge. Cheese is an alkali, so it's excellent at neutralising the foods we have already eaten.

There are certain dos and don'ts for cheeses. Always remember to take your cheeses out of the fridge a couple of hours before you intend to eat them, bringing them up to room temperature. But make a judgement on it as some cheeses need less time. So, ideally, take them out gradually depending on how hard or soft they are.

Cut your cheese into pre-portioned pieces, this prevents any leftover cheese that you may end saving looking like a smashed pile of goo. Don't leave the smelly cheese in the dining area where the aromas might affect your guests' experience of tasting their wine and other food. Let them ripen and soften in the kitchen. Many of those suitable wines for cheese will mirror the wines for dessert; however there are a select few that are just sublime with a hearty cheeseboard. The most important thing to remember here is there is no one size fits all. Just because it's a red wine, this does not mean it will pair with every cheese. The same can be said for white wine also. So, if you have a certain wine in mind, try and select the cheeses based around this, as shown in the table below.

Soft cheeses (Brie, Camembert or goat's cheese)	Sauvignon Blanc, unoaked Chardonnay or a bone-dry Riesling (they are quite acidic so wine to match the acidity levels is required) – Vignerons de Valencay Loire Sauvignon Blanc
Blue cheese (Cashel Blue, Stilton, Roquefort or Gorgonzola)	Ruby port (the saltiness needs to be tamed by sweetness and the extra weight in this wine, and the fine sweet notes of dried fruits are well able for these mouldy salty cheeses) – Osborne Ruby Port
Hard cheeses (Parmesan, vintage Cheddar, Comte or Manchego)	Cabernet Sauvignon, Rioja Reserva or Nebbiolo (they have gripping tannins that absolutely love the proteins in hard cheese and so they melt away) – De Marie Nebbiolo d'Alba
Soft, gooey fondue-style heated cheese (raclette)	Muscadet or Sauvignon Blanc (lighter, steelier wines cut through all the richness) – Muscadet Sur Lie, Nicolas Reau 'La Pentiere'

Chapter 7

Fizztivites: A Gander at Sparkling Wines

> *Did you know?*
> *Women are more susceptible to the effects of*
> *wine than men. And this is due to our biology!*
> *Women have fewer enzymes in the stomach lining*
> *required to break down alcohol than men.*

I remember working in a high-end restaurant in the mid 2000s, long after I had completed my studies. Because of the unabashed greed and gluttony of the time, my specific wine studies were as useful as a chocolate teapot. People would have drunk wine out of a smelly welly – all manners and grace had left this city.

The restaurant I worked in, located in the heart of Dublin, had a client list that would make your eyes water. Black company credit cards were thrown around like plastic bags in the wind. Little regard was paid to the totals of the bills, crass to even check. Credit-card slips were signed without even a glance, as a selection of American crooners sang through the speakers.

The wine list was Bible-length, bursting with Bordeaux and Burgundy wines of course. Fine-crystal Champagne flutes tinkled, accompanied by raucous laughter and celebrations. It was Fossett's Circus, fuelled by Dom Pérignon and Château Lynch-Bages. High-heeled Jimmy Choos trotted around the rooms gallantly, as buttons burst on fine suits with the weight of Béarnaise and dry-aged ribeyes. It was some time to be alive for sure.

I was part of the steerage crew. My peers and I were dressed as penguins, with dark waistcoats and hideously long white aprons, and armed with wine openers, razor-sharp wit and an ability to filter through the vulgarity. Part of the bargain for making outlandish tips was to succumb to the outlandish requests of our nouveau-riche punters. It suited us guerrilla waiters to be fair.

On this one occasion, the tipsiest woman in Ireland ordered a bottle of Cristal 2002. After discussing with my manager whether we should serve her or not, her merry friend assured us she was fine. Selfishly, I was looking forward to opening a bottle of such calibre, so I trundled on with the mission at hand. By the time my fellow penguin sommelier had located the bottle, our lovely lady friend had perked up a bit. I peeled off the yellow sleeve and pulled out the glistening bottle, as Dean Martin chirped away in the background. I unwrapped the foil at the top, and proceeded to unwind the copper wire that clasped the mushroom cork. If I'm honest, at the time I was a little inexperienced to be opening a bottle of vintage Champagne, but God loves a trier.

Just as I removed the wire, a lofty, swaying punter fell over and bumped into my shoulder, and off popped the cork. It flew straight into my eye socket. Boom! My legs went from underneath me. I'm told the bottle spun out of control onto the floor, spewing vintage Champagne violently into the air. I was too busy clinging to my eye socket after the full force of a 32 kmph cork flew into it. Then the realisation set in. Morto!

I was quick to jump back up and try and salvage the bottle, but it was currently under table twelve, where a builder-developer-type was entertaining his family. They became soaked, as the bottle spun ferociously. I was losing my mind at this stage. A flood of penguins rushed to the scene to halt the chaos. Too late, that sparkling train had left the station and it was gushing bubbles everywhere.

Eventually, the tsunami of Cristal stopped raging. Eventually, the bottle was handed over by the lovely wife of the builder, with a half-smile and a look of bemusement. I skulked off into the staff quarters and wept. Not only did I have a whopping shiner, my ego was just as bruised. I was stunned. In later years, I reflected: the absolute cheek of me to think I could chance my arm at opening a bottle of vintage Champagne that had had years of transporting and ageing. You never take the wire off the cork without holding the cork down with your other hand. Never!

Or else be prepared for the chaos.

It will be no huge shock for you to learn that the sparkling-wine category has exploded in the past ten years globally. Supermarket shelves are now tightly packed with mushroom-corked bottles, and restaurants and bars are beefing up their bubbles section of the menu. In fact, both production and consumption of these effervescent wines has grown by a whopping 57 per cent since 2012. What was once a smaller sector of the market, at a meagre 5 per cent, is now escalating year on year to a far more respectable 10 per cent of the global market share of wine production.

We can likely attribute most of the successes and newfound appetite for sparkling wines to Proseccos. These styles of wine filled a gaping hole in the market for a more affordable bubble in our glass. Many of us are still not at the scale where we are swilling fine vintage Champagnes on a random Tuesday. Thankfully, the advent of these vibrant and cheeky affordable Proseccos opened the floodgates to a selection of top-quality, more-affordable sparkling wines from France, Spain, Germany and England.

This is one of my favourite chapters because I absolutely love sparkling wines. I don't know what it is, but I reckon it's because of the infrequency with which I drink them. I seem to only buy a bottle of bubbles when it's a Friday or a treat-type scenario. And I often wonder to myself, why? It's literally the exact same wine, only with bubbles in it. In today's climate, there are very affordable bottles of bubbles with decent examples coming in at €13 or €14. Sure, listen, it's for nothing.

So, what makes them so special? Why do 95 per cent of the

population get excited when they see a bottle of bubbly coming to the table? What is the magic, the mystique, the giddiness all about?

> *Top tip*
> *Remember, bubbles should be drunk cold. The cooler temperatures keep the bubbles fresher for longer. So to turbo chill a bottle, wet a sheet of kitchen paper and wrap it around the bottle. Put the bottle into the freezer and let it rest for ten minutes. When you take the bottle out, it will be at the optimum chilled temperature.*

Opening a bottle with bubbles in it

So now that I have divulged one of my most embarrassing moments to you, I'm here to tell you what I've learned from my mistakes. There's a professional way to open a bottle of sparkling wine, and I will lay out the directions here.

All sparkling wine bottles are heavy, with a large punt (the dent in the bottom of the bottle that strengthens it) and a wire protecting the cork that is squashed into the bottle. This is because there's over three bars of atmospheric pressure in the bottle. In the likes of a well-made fine Champagne, you can have up to six bars of pressure. In layman's terms, a car tyre has one bar of atmospheric pressure.

This means your average bottle of Cava, Crémant or Champagne has three times the pressure of your car tyres.

The energetic levels of CO_2 in the bottles means opening them comes with a warning. According to *Decanter* magazine, a German scientist Friedrich Black once logged a cork flying out of a bottle of Champagne at 40kmph/28 mph. This cork can travel to your eye in less than 0.5 seconds, making this a real danger to yourself – and speaking from direct experience, it is no joke.

Following the points below and on the next page when opening a bottle of Champagne will help with a smoother opening and lower the chances of an ol' eye gouge. Remember, if the bottle has been vigorously shaken, the trapped CO_2 will make things worse. So, take care.

1. Always carry the bottle at a tilted forty-five-degree angle.
2. With one hand placed firmly on the bottom of the bottle, begin to peel back the foil at the top.
3. Still holding the bottom of the bottle, begin to unravel the wire that's around the cork.
4. Loosen the wire whilst keeping a finger on the top of the bottle, all the while still holding the bottom of the bottle.
5. As you loosen the wire and the cork, start to twist the bottom of the bottle.
6. Keep the top of the bottle firmly in one position in your hand. Do not move the top of the bottle.
7. Continue to turn the bottom of the bottle. You will feel the pressure build up.

8. As you twist the bottle very slowly, push against the force of the CO_2.

9. When you feel the cork has become loose from the neck of the bottle, you will feel the biggest push, but try to keep the bottle still.

10. Release the cork slowly. You should hear a 'whooosh' sound as opposed to a 'pop'. Why? A whoosh sounds means you've manged to retain more of the CO_2 in the bottle, therefore your bubbles will stay in the wine for longer.

Some interesting facts about Champagne and sparkling wines:

1. There are over 49 million bubbles in a 750ml bottle of Champagne. That equates to over 7 million bubbles per glass.

2. A standard glass of Champagne emits 30 bubbles every second.

3. Marilyn Monroe famously took a bath in Champagne. It took 350 bottles to fill her bath.

4. The first glass of any sparkling wine poured has the most bubbles. This means the alcohol in the wine gets into your bloodstream more quickly, so, effectively, the first glass poured is the most potent.

5. The most expensive bottle of wine made costs $2.07 million. It was designed by Alexander Amosu and Swarovski, handcrafted from 18-carat solid gold, with a deep-cut 19-carat white diamond at its centre. Naturally, the bottle is the most expensive part.

6. About 28,000 bottles of Champagne are served at Wimbledon every year.

7. The Romans enjoyed their own local bubbles called Prosecco for centuries; however it was not until the nineteenth century, when Carpenè Moltovi subjected the wine to a second fermentation, that a stronger presence of tiny bubbles began to appear and create the wine as we know it today.

8. The UK consumes a third of the volume of Prosecco consumed each year across the globe. That's 420 million bottles.

9. In 2016, there was a shortage of the grape Glera that is used for Prosecco production. Such was the drastic shortage that all Prosecco was pulled from the shelves of Sainsburys due to excessive demands.

10. A flute-shaped glass will circulate the bubbles to retain them better in the glass; however a wine glass is preferable for vintage Champagne so you can also smell the aromas. The vintage style 'Marie Antoinette' coupe glasses are beautiful to look at, but are terrible at retaining the bubbles.

Origins of bubbles

Much like the beginnings of wine, many a fable is told of who invented bubbles in wine. The suave and clever marketeers in the region of Champagne in northern France would have you believe that the Benedictine monk Dom Pérignon was the first to create bubbles. It has been stated that he was 'seeing stars in his wine', referring to the bubbles. But like 'Goldilocks and the Three Bears' or 'Snow White', the fable is the magical part, and not necessarily the truth.

It suits the celebrious region of Champagne to have a mythical beginning to their most-prized possession. It creates the narrative to suggest that bubbles were created by accident by a mystical monk, who spearheaded the campaign of nouveau sparkling wine production. This is just not true. The beginnings of trapping bubbles in wine are far less exciting and magical, yet still very interesting.

So, let's have a look.

Sparkling wines have been prevalent throughout the world since the seventeenth and eighteenth centuries, intentionally or not. Bubbles occur in the wine when the fermentation process creates carbon dioxide as a by-product and this is trapped. As we know by now, when yeasts react with the sugars in the liquid, they create alcohol and carbon dioxide.

**Yeasts + Sugars =
Alcohol + Carbon Dioxide**

So sparkling wine can be made by trapping in the bottle the initial CO_2 that's made. Or sugar is added to a still wine, the yeasts react once more for a second fermentation, and a wine with a generous bubble count is created.

How bubbles are made

There are a variety of ways to make bubbles in your wine.

Ancestral method/pétillant-naturel (pét-nat)

As the name suggests, this is the oldest form of production. Basically, the wine is removed from the tank before the full fermentation process has finished, so the remaining carbon dioxide that is produced is contained within the bottle. Very often, these wines are left unfiltered by their natural-driven producers, leaving cloudy wines. These are really lovely wines for a summer's day with a charcuterie or cheeseboard. They have a light, bubbly feel, with plenty of fruit aromas and a generous finish.

Examples: There are fantastic pét-nat's from the south of France and some beautiful ones from Portugal. Some examples might be Folias de Baco Uivo (Portugal), Domaine Albert de Conti (France) and Sardinita pét-nat (Portugal).

Traditional method

This is also commonly referred to as the Champagne method/ Méthode Champenoise as it was first derived there. It is the most common form of creating bubbles in a wine and is certainly the most labour-intensive method, and the wines are the longest lived and highest quality.

This process involves a second fermentation that takes place inside the bottle that the wine will be sold in. This second fermentation is stimulated by the addition of 'liqueur de tirage' (yeasts, sugar and wine) to the bottle. After the yeasts have finished working and have died off, they drop to the bottom of the bottle. These dead yeast cells remain in contact with the wine, as the wine bottles are turned two millimetres per day. This ensures the yeast cells have an opportunity to come in contact with all of the wine within the bottle. This period is called 'lees ageing'.

- Champagne requires at least two years' lees ageing.
- Crémant requires at least one year's ageing.
- Cava requires at least one year's lees ageing.
- Prosecco Spumante requires at least nine months' lees ageing.

The longer the wine is left on the lees to age, the more aromas and flavours are picked up. Classic Champagne aromas are digestive biscuits, apricot pastry and brioche. These are aromas directly derived from those yeast cells.

As Champagne has to be aged by law for two years, these flavours are more commonly associated with these wines. However, if a top-quality Cava or Prosecco is aged for longer than their one-year period, they may also start to develop some of those classic biscuity aromas and flavours. The base limit for ageing Cava is one year by law and Prosecco is nine months' lees ageing, and if the producer has spent more time and more money ageing their wines, there may be a reference to that on the back label.

After the required ageing period, the lees will be removed by a process called riddling. This is a gentle process where the bottles are still turned two millimetres a day to ensure the dead yeasts cells come in contact with all of the wine, but the wines are placed upside down (at a forty-five-degree angle) on wooden boards. The yeast travels down through the bottle, eventually to the neck of the bottle, flavouring the wine as it goes. The upside-down bottles are frozen at the neck, and this helps to remove the solid block of yeast cells that just pops out.

At this stage, a minute mix of sugar and wine called the dosage is added. The final cork is squashed in, the wire is bound, and the foil cover is chosen.

Examples: Champagne, Cava, Prosecco Spumante and Asti

Charmat method/tank method

This is a far less costly way of making sparkling wine. It is sometimes called the tank method because this is where the secondary fermentation takes place. The 'liqueur de tirage' is added to the tank so, logically, this means there is less contact with the lees and therefore a lower volume of bubbles, larger bubbles and less of the biscuity-pastry flavours you achieve from ageing a wine on the lees.

The tank is chilled, and the secondary fermentation stops.

This method creates clean, fruity flavours rather than complex savoury pastry notes. And that's fine for everyday sparkling wines that are consumed without foods or perhaps used in summery-style cocktails.

There's a huge place on the market for these very affordable sparkling wines, recognisable from their screwcap closure. No cork is required as the pressure is far lower because there are fewer and lighter bubbles. Just a simple twist of the cap is needed to open these wines.

Examples: German Sekt, Prosecco Frizzante, Asti Spumante

Transfer method

This is a combination of both bottle and tank. The wine undergoes secondary fermentation in the bottle with the lees. And then the wines are transferred into a pressurised tank, the sediments are left to filter to the bottom, and the liquid is transferred back into the bottles. This enables flavours and characters to emerge from the yeast cells, whilst also speeding up the normally lengthy riddling process. This method is often used on larger-size bottles.

Examples: magnums, jeroboam, etc.

History of creating bubbles in wine

Everyone believes that the French invented sparkling wine, but the Italians and the Spanish were also creating effervescent wines in the 1700s and 1800s. Truthfully, though, the first documentations of sparkling wines are from the region in the south of France called Limoux. Here, the monks of Saint-Hilaire documented their daily escapades and within this was the discovery of bubbles in a wine in the year 1531. Naturally, this wine would have been made in the ancestral method, and possibly was a complete accident. They may have bottled the wine, then the temperature dropped and so the fermentation stopped. As the weather warmed up again, the fermentation restarted, thus creating natural bubbles inside of the bottle.

Periods of production times

1500s	Limoux
1700s	Dom Pérignon
1754	Col Fondo Prosecco
1872	Josep Raventós Cava (Cordoníu)

Champagne

The first evidence of winemaking in this northern French wine region is back in the sixth century. The Church was heavily involved here, especially the Benedictine monks, including one Dom Pérignon. Although he may not have invented bubbles in wine, he was certainly instrumental in bringing the findings in Limoux back up to Champagne. Furthermore, he was very influential in creating this blended style of wine (see p.91) that is still used to this day.

Champagne is one region today that still permits blending

from year to year. These wines are called non-vintage (NV). This region was also the first in France to classify this term.

Making Champagne is a delicate balance, and the location of the region in northern France further adds to its difficulties. The ideal weather for grape growing is not a given each year and can be very unpredictable. Therefore, winemakers are allowed to blend the wines from a poor vintage with those from previous years that may have had more favourable weather.

Up until 1690, all wines from France were known as 'French wine'. From that point on, any wine produced in this region was known as 'Champagne wine'.

Advances in glass production evolved as the seventeenth century progressed. Up until this point, the glass bottles kept smashing under the pressure of the trapped CO_2. It was nicknamed 'the Devil's wine'. The English were influential in the glass trade and created a sturdy-enough glass bottle to withstand the pressure. The punt in the bottom was added to reinforce the strength of the bottle. This enabled the wines to become even more popular. The first Champagne houses opened stores in the local cities of Reims, Aÿ and Épernay.

Dom Pérignon passed away in 1715, just as the rise of Champagne had started. Credit lies with the Champagne house of Ruinart, who, in 1729, were the first Champagne house to begin shipping their effervescent styles across Europe. This style of wine was gaining traction amongst the bourgeoisie, especially Europe's royal families. In 1745, Moët et Chandon became the first sparkling wine in the court of King Louis XV.

By 1772, the area was experiencing comfortable success, yet there were improvements happening all the time. Madame Clicquot (of Veuve Clicquot) is famous for inventing the riddling process explained on p.179.

The success of this region and its wines was also due to proximity to the city of Reims, where the kings were anointed for each coronation. Naturally, the local wines were sampled to celebrate the incoming kings. So began the association with Champagne and celebrations.

As the nineteenth century came to a close, the producers and Champagne houses were well aware of their high-end, celebrious product. By 1887, they were successful in a bid to claim the name Champagne exclusively for their wines.

By 1936, the regional quality assurance system in France, the appellation contrôlée, had delineated and certified the region as Champagne appellation origine contrôlée (Champagne AOC). Strict rules were laid down that local producers had to adhere to. The name is associated with glamour, prestige, luxury and opulence, and the savvy producers of this region intended to protect their name to the highest courts in the land.

According to the official Champagne website, during the 1960s a 'Spanish Champagne' went on sale in a store in England, and it was in fact the British High Court that ruled against it, claiming Champagne was an original French product. This set a precedent for countries worldwide preventing them from selling sparkling wines under the term Champagne. For many a decade, people had believed this was the official term for a sparkling wine and not the actual name of the region the wine was produced in.

There have been countless cases brought to the EU Court of Justice for products that have adapted the name in their title, like sorbets, beers, perfumes and colours of paints. However, all are unsuccessful. The French go above and beyond to protect this precious term. The most recent ruling was in 2021, when a Spanish tapas bar was using the name Champanillo. The EU Court of Justice ruled in favour of the French and the owners of the tapas bar reluctantly changed its name.

Crémant

There are eight other regions in France that produce serious-quality sparkling wines without the high price tag, yet still possessing all the flavour and bubbles. These eight regions are legally allowed to classify and call their wines 'Crémant', which means creamy.

The term was originally used in the Champagne region to classify a lower effervescent wine. But when the term 'Champagne' was outlawed for wines made outside the region, the trade-off was the term 'Crémant'.

Crémant was originally a way of using grapes whose acidity was too high for still wines. It is a style of wine that embraces diversity and uniqueness, as each region has their own permitted grape varieties. Therefore, the flavours of these wines vary. They do, however, have common parameters for quality they must adhere to. All grapes must be hand harvested. Ageing limits are equal in terms of twelve months minimum

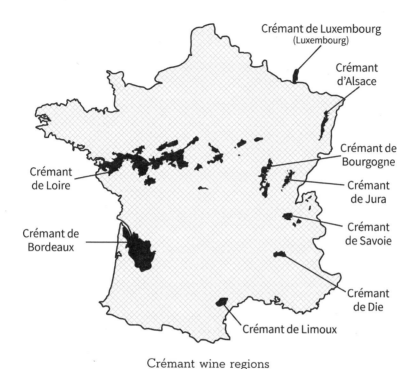

Crémant wine regions

of lees ageing for any Crémant. And the same amount of dosage (mix of sugar and wine) must be added to the wines before bottling.

Stylistically, these wines range from a light, easy-drinking summery sparkler to a toasty, creamy, rich wine that mirrors fine Champagne.

Crémant d'Alsace, Jura and Savoie tend to be more neutral in style, and these are made from Pinot Blanc (Alsace), Savagnin (Jura) and Jacquère and Chardonnay (Savoie).

For similarities to the famous Champagne wines, Crémant de Bourgogne would be the closest. But only because they use the same grapes (Chardonnay, Pinot Noir and Pinot Munier). Such is the demand for Crémant now, Jean Charles Boisset, one of Bourgogne's most widely recognised producers, claims his production is over 27 per cent of all his wines. The region itself is investing and producing over 18 million bottles a year.

The likes of Crémant de Bourgogne have even stricter rules again. They must hand harvest their grapes in whole bunches and in perforated boxes, whilst exercising the same pressing protocols as the Champagne region. Furthermore, it is law to declare your vineyard for Crémant production before the end of March. Your vines must not be used as an afterthought – or worse still as an economical solution to use up all your surplus supply of juice. These are serious wines that are produced using a classic Champagne method, whereby a still wine has a dose of sugar and yeast added to the bottle and is left to age for twelve to eighteen months. Meticulous care is taken to turn these bottles once daily, very minimally, and this way the yeast can react with of all the liquid to create the carbon dioxide to form well over 20 million bubbles per bottle!

However, the main difference between choosing a Crémant de Bourgogne over a Champagne would be a far lower price tag because even though they have a long ageing process that creates those fine, tiny bubbles, the wines will never be aged as long as the minimum age for Champagne, which is two years.

Full varietal Pinot Noir is used here too to make sleek and soft rosé sparkling wines. A wine like this can partner such a staggering array of foods, you would be shocked. It's perfect for Asian dishes.

A fruitier version is Crémant de Loire, in which they use Chenin Blanc and some Pinot Noir for summery rosé bubbles. The producers use Chenin Blanc to give flavours of lemons, quince and honey. Producers like Bollinger and Deutz have a firm presence here, making some stellar wines. Crémant de Limoux is also made using Chenin Blanc, and therefore has a riper fruit to it.

Crémant de Bordeaux is one of the more unique regions for sparkling as they permit five grapes (Sauvignon Blanc, Sémillon, Muscadelle, Merlot and Cabernet Franc) to be used in production. The flavours and styles can vary greatly. However, they are a little more difficult to find as most producers in this region tend to focus all their efforts on still wine production. A must though if you can get your hands on them here in Ireland.

And why choose a Crémant?

Because the modern consumer is becoming far more astute about the option of buying sparkling wines with supreme quality and style for a fraction of the price tag. These wines can offer all of the fanfare of a Champagne, with tiny bubbles, many varying flavours to suit all palates and an ability to suit a wide range of foods and rich dishes. Crémant wines are finally having their day for sure now!

Cava

Cava is the Spanish word for 'cellar', and it is here that all Cava must be aged for at least one year, though many quality-driven producers will age their wines beyond a year, and some even as long as five years.

Its origins began in the north-western wine region of Penedès in Catalonia. A group of devastated wine producers decided to come together after a vine louse ripped through their vineyards and decimated their vines. In the mid 1800s, they decided to re-crop the vineyards with white grapes that were more suitable than the previous red grapes. A gentlemen called José Raventós had just come back from his visit to Champagne and was inspired. They planted Macabeo, Xarel·lo and Parellada – three white grapes that thrived in the local soils and enjoyed the area's Mediterranean climate.

Over time, similar to the rest of the Spanish wine industry, quality levels have been improved through major research and development. In 1904, the visit of King Alfonso to Penedès signified the recognition of this region as a quality-driven producer of sparkling wines for Spain. The first time the term Cava was documented was in 1959, and it became the official name for sparkling wine from this region. Two major producers that dominated the market in the past were Cordoníu and Freixenet. Now there are over 206 producers that highlight the quality and diversity of this truly industrious region.

There is now a new designation which involves adhering to even stricter rules of quality, such as hand harvesting, purely organic or biodynamic grapes, a minimum eighteen months of ageing and only using permitted grapes. This designation is called 'Corpinnat', and these producers are travelling the globe to market and promote their special wines.

Cava is the most exported wine in Spain and is actually the highest volume exported wine in the world at a whopping 200 million bottles a year.

Prosecco

This Italian sparkling wine has been one of the most successful wines to ever grace the Italian shores. It has a long and illustrious history spanning centuries of adoration for this light, fruity and accessible sparkling wine. It is perfect as an aperitif, but also idyllic with salty hams and creamy cheese.

Nevertheless, this wine also has a raucous reputation.

The quality levels vary like a rollercoaster track: wild and hard to predict. A wine can be labelled as Prosecco but have the taste profile of a leftover can of rotten peas. OK, that may bit a harsh, but the varying levels of quality in Prosecco can be shocking, so let's try and clear some of that up.

The first documentation of the name Prosecco dates back to the end of the sixteenth century. Nobile Vino Pucinum created a wine that was named after the nearby Castello di Prosecco. This was in the region Trieste, in Friuli-Venezia Giulia, right in the north-east of Italy, which to this day is still one of the country's finer quality wine-making regions.

Giacomo Puccini, an Italian opera composer, was a huge fan of these wines, giving them a degree of notoriety at the time. Heading towards the end of the eighteenth century, vines were

Prosecco region

spreading down as far as the winemaking region Veneto, which is the homestead of Prosecco in today's world.

In 1868, Antonio Carpenè, who was a prolific winemaker, would often mention, promote and show appreciation for Prosecco, which contributed to the wine being developed widespread across Italy. He went on to set up a wine school in Conegliano-Valdobbiadene. These names are now famous globally for high-end Prosecco.

In 2009, these two Prosecco sub-regions received the coveted classification, which is Italy's highest, the DOCG (Denominazione di Origine Controllata e Garantita). A further nine provinces in the north-east of Italy received the next level down of DOC (Denominazione di Origine).

Prosecco has seen growth year-on-year, and most specifically, 2003 was the first year for Prosecco to outsell Champagne globally.

Because of the ever-increasing demand for an affordable, everyday sparkling wine, the Italians have moved a vast proportion of production from bottle fermentation to tank fermentation. This ultimately speeds up the process and enables the region to keep up with demands.

Prosecco *Frizzante* is tank fermented and is known for its screwcap or bottle-cap closure. The bubbles are far lighter and often the wine can be flat by the end of your glass. Very handy for use in cocktails or in restaurants and bars looking for a cheap wine by the glass. It usually retails from €7.99 to €12.99.

Prosecco *Spumante* are the wines that are bottle fermented. This means they are aged for nine months at least in the bottle; therefore, the bubbles will be far more pronounced, and it might even stay fresh two or three days if you pop the bottle back into the fridge again. These wines are usually on average €4 to €5 more expensive and are the perfect example of stretching your budget a little further to enable you to enjoy a different quality level when it comes to the wine.

Style and flavours

Region	Crémant	Cava	Prosecco	Champagne	Vintage Champagne
Grapes	Chardonnay, Cabernet Franc, Pinot Meunier, Chenin Blanc, Pinot Blanc	Macabeo, Xarel-lo	Glera	Chardonnay, Pinot Noir, Macabeo	Chardonnay, Pinot Noir, Pinot Meunier
Production	Traditional method	Traditional method	Tank method	Traditional method	Traditional method
Ageing period	1 year	1 year	9 months (Spumante)	2 years	5 years plus
Flavours	Lemons, tangerines, rhubarb, brioche and canned strawberries	Quince, citrus fruits, white flowers	Peach, apricot	Baked lemons, honey, peach frangipane, glazed strawberries, mushroom, toasted almonds	Lemon tart, clementines, Key lime pie, marzipan, mushroom, crushed hazelnuts
Foods	Salami, oysters, popcorn, bacon and cabbage	Chorizo, Parma ham, popcorn	Buttered toast, hard cheeses, peanuts, honey	Liver pâté, oysters, smoked almonds	Pâté, shellfish, roast duck, smoked trout, game meats
Alcohol levels	12%	11–12.5%	10–11%	12.5%	12%
Price Range	€25+	€15–€25	€8–€25	€30–€65	€80+

Chapter 8

Sip-sational Wine Gadgets and Glassware

Did you know?
The standard bottle of wine holds 750
millilitres of wine but other sizes exist.

Spilt/Piccolo (187.5ml - quarter bottle)

Half/Demi (350ml - half a bottle)

Jennie (500ml - 0.66 bottle)

Magnum (1.5l - 2 standards bottles)

Double Magnum (3l - 4 standard bottles)

Jeroboam (4.5l - 6 standard bottles)

Imperial (6l - 8 standard bottles)

Salmanazar (9l - 12 standard bottles)

Balthazar (12l - 16 standard bottles)

Nebuchadnezzar (15l - 20 standard bottles)

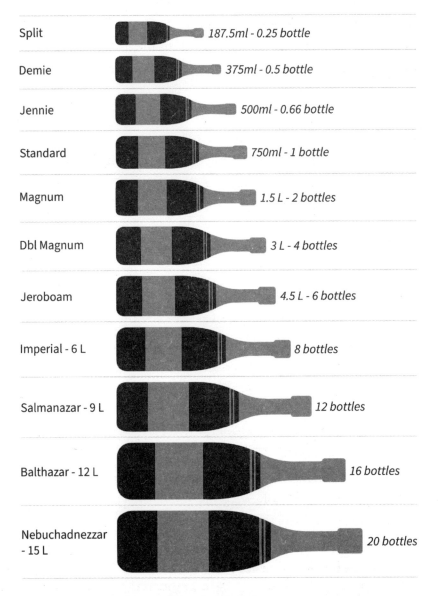

Split		187.5ml - 0.25 bottle
Demie		375ml - 0.5 bottle
Jennie		500ml - 0.66 bottle
Standard		750ml - 1 bottle
Magnum		1.5 L - 2 bottles
Dbl Magnum		3 L - 4 bottles
Jeroboam		4.5 L - 6 bottles
Imperial - 6 L		8 bottles
Salmanazar - 9 L		12 bottles
Balthazar - 12 L		16 bottles
Nebuchadnezzar - 15 L		20 bottles

Wine bottle sizes

It was a muggy Saturday evening in late September. I was well into my wine career and I was working as the head sommelier in one of the finest hotels in Ireland. In terms of prestige, experience and the opportunity to taste fine wines, it was the absolute pinnacle.

The wine list was a viticultural tome, with the gargantuan presence of a sumo wrestler. I often used it as a method to quieten those people who thought they knew more than anyone else in the room. This massive maroon book was the game-changer. As I placed the book on the table's fresh, crisp white linen, I would chuckle to myself and think of that classic humbling Irish phrase, 'now this will soften your cough for you'!

Anyway, back to this fateful Saturday-evening service. The dining room was bursting - there was a deluge of guests - it was one of the busiest services I had witnessed. This rather unassuming New Yorker glided into the restaurant and sat down at his table for one. It was a minute or two before I got to him to introduce myself and slide over the winelist. It took him less than a minute to navigate his way to the section on Bordeaux wines and boom - he chose the most expensive wine on the list, a Château Cheval Blanc 1961. An iconic wine from an even more iconic vintage. It took all my might to play it cool.

I sprinted to the cellar during the busiest service ever. Our dark, cool cellar was not normally frequented during service, but this was an exceptional circumstance. This was a moment in time. A bottle of history was waiting to be opened. This charmed first-growth Bordeaux had waited a meagre fifty years to be opened. And it felt fitting opening this bottle on its fiftieth birthday and I felt very honoured as I peeled back the foil. It wasn't the easiest to remove, but the power of adrenalin was keeping me sane.

There was a flurry of excitement gathering around me as word spread. At this stage, the hotel's general manager had come down to see the craic. I was trembling. And then disaster! I broke the cork in the bottle. Oh sweet Jesus, the nerves were too much. I managed to compose myself and rescue the broken cork from the bottle. I then poured the wine through a muslin cloth to remove any unwanted pieces of cork. I beamed at the New Yorker as I proudly poured his ruby-coloured liquid gold. He toasted to the whole dining room, and who would blame him. He had spent the guts of €2,500 on his bottle. He offered me a small glass and I absolutely took it. I could hear the choir sounds of 'hallelujah' ringing in my head. I did it, I got the chance to taste a 1961 iconic Bordeaux. I didn't care after that what he did with his wine. He could've poured it on his chips if he wanted.

But what happened next was completely unexpected.

I had turned my back for one second and when I looked at him again, I noticed he had poured the whole decanter of wine into his fine-crystal Riedel balloon glass. I howled internally. I skipped away giggling. It was the funniest thing. Never have I had more respect for anyone who chooses to live life the way they want. I was glad, though, that I had chosen the perfect glass for the job: a bloody big finely spun crystal goblet from Riedel that has the charm and charisma to carry off a 1961 Bordeaux.

Top tip
Don't let anyone sway your wine choices. If
you like the wine, then it's a good-quality
wine as far as you are concerned. We have
no time for wine snobbery in this gang.

The creativity, ingenuity and adaptivity of winemakers has long been a global wonder, challenging themselves each year to produce the wines that fill our glasses no matter what Mother Nature throws at them.

Most other industries are battling against the financial markets or the consumer market or the property market, but the wine industry has to work with nature and overcome its challenges, be it climate change or natural disaster. I for one take my hat off to them and their endless pursuit of perfection. We are gifted with so many incredible wines that have the most impressive backstories.

Winemaking is storytelling at its finest. Each grape, each barrel, each cuvée is filled with passion, love and hope. And when the forces of nature come down upon them, these winemakers show their true skill. Wine is a honey that binds us together through cultural and racial differences. So, when I order a glass of wine in a bar and it is served in a tumbler that could survive an atomic bomb, my heart dips a little.

The efforts and skill of the winemaker deserve to be recognised and a bathroom toothbrush glass is just not going to cut the mustard. The thick rim of a glass like this makes sure you miss half of your tastebuds at the tip of your tongue. The wide opening ensures all the delicate, hard-fought-after aromas are lost amongst the cologne- and perfumed-filled air in the bar you have ordered your wine in. I know it is important to look the part and to hang with the Gen Z kids looking cool, but drinking wine out of a tin is just not what the doctor ordered. And let me tell you, it won't show off the wine to its full glory.

With that in mind, let's have a little look at glassware and gadgets that will.

| C1670 | C1750 | C1859 | C1980s | C1990s |

Wine glasses through history

Glassware

Glassware is possibly one of the most crucial elements to elevating your wine experience. It is what holds your wine, of course, but it can also highlight nuances in your wine. Wine glasses have increased in size almost seven-fold over the last 300 years, almost doubling in size in the past twenty years alone.

Glass wine vessels were first documented in Egyptian culture as far back as 1500 BCE. The road has been long and varied to get to where we are today, where glass blowers create wine glasses that suit particular grapes and crystal is spun so thin the rim of the glass melts into your tongue. Naturally, you pay for these luxuries. A single stem can set you back over €120.

There have been copious studies on glassware and how they impact flavours. A recent study by Greg Hirson at University of California, Davis, concluded that, in fact, there are major differences between different shaped glasses. Hirson stated that the perception of the wine drinker was important to the taste of wine too. Meaning that if we are drinking from a fine wine glass with delicate features, this should open up our minds and our perceptions to noticing more flavours from the wine.

Glassware aids the overall ergonomic and sensory experience, but you will be glad to know you don't have to spend a ludicrous amount of money on a wine glass – there are plenty of good value examples out there. Factors like functionality, design, price and how easy it is to clean should be at the forefront of your mind when you are choosing some glassware. You really know you're an adult when you have a full set of six white-wine glasses, red-wine glasses and maybe even a set of Champagne flutes.

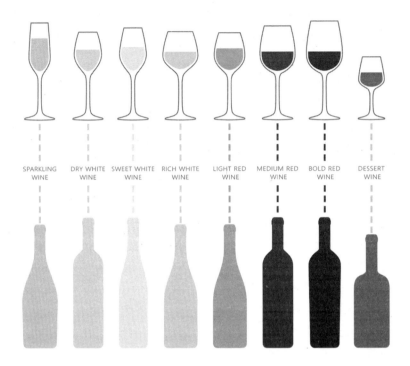

Different wine glass sizes

Reidel

This is a famous Austrian crystal company that has been in business for eleven generations. This company is synonymous with quality in restaurants, wineries and with sommeliers the world over. They specialise in making fine-crystal glassware, decanters, perfume bottles and chandeliers.

It was Claus Josef Riedel that altered the company from making traditional colourful glassware to minimal, unadorned, thin-blown crystal glassware during the second half of the twentieth century. He elevated the glass into a new era of sleek design that was backed up by research and development. His first range of glassware based on the flavours of wine was called the Sommeliers range and was met with rave reviews. Some of their most dynamic and value-driven ranges are the Vinum range and the Performance range. Neither are cheap, but they are a complete experience to drink from.

The rim of a Riedel glass is so thin it seamlessly channels the wine to flow directly on to your tongue, arriving at the exact tastebuds required to pick up the flavours in the wine.

In the Vinum range, the bowl of the Cabernet Sauvignon glass is far wider and broader than the bowl for the Riesling glass because of the structure of Cabernet, which has dark thick skins, therefore there are big tannins in the wine. The Vinum range includes glass bowl shapes suited for specific grape varieties. The bowl of the glass widens to enable maximum swirling.

The Riesling grape has a far thinner skin and higher acidity levels, therefore the bowl of the glass is smaller to keep the gentler aromas and flavours intact and delivered straight to the nose through a far narrower opening. It's a complete indulgent experience drinking wine from a glass like this, and if you're a wine lover you should treat yourself once in your life.

You can buy the Vinum range direct on the Riedel website for €49 for a pair.

The Performance range of Riedel glasses are the cat's pyjamas, or however you refer to something that is decadent and lush. These finely spun crystal glasses have grooves in them. Riedel themselves describe these glasses as an ultimate loudspeaker for fine wine. The bowls have a light-optic impact, which means little to me, but speaking from the experience of drinking from these glasses, the grooves add more of a surface area to the glass, which means that, after one swirl, the wine has considerably opened up.

It is worth noting that all these Riedel glasses are labelled as dishwasher safe, however I tend to hand wash mine. Please take care though if following my example. I remember working as a sommelier in one of Ireland's finest hotels. I was polishing one of these glasses and the stem broke. The crystal stem was so sharp it sliced my finger open. I had to get seven stitches on my finger and the doctor commented it must have been a very sharp object that cut my finger because the wound was so clean. So be very, very careful when cleaning these beautiful glasses.

A pair of these glasses in the grape varietal of your choice will set you back €59.

Zalto

Another Austrian glass company that speaks of absolute decadence and a memorable experience drinking wine from is Zalto.

Zalto Denk'Art glasses have been described as the Olympic gymnast in the wine-glass arena. They are so light it is hard to imagine. You feel like your bare hand will crush them. They have an extremely fine rim with a long, thin, delicate stem that contrasts beautifully with the wide bowl. The bowl is measured in accordance with the tilt of the earth. With measurements of

24, 48 and 72 degrees, this creates 'cosmic parallels' and, to us mere mortals, it means the wine will bounce off the glass and the flavours will taste smoother.

In reality, these are the types of glass that are left in the cupboard if your children are in the room or if your friend is over and they've already had a few pints in the pub. These glasses are for the ultimate wine-drinking occasion, perhaps with a friend, where much thought and adulation are adorned upon the chosen wine you are drinking. These finely spun crystal creations are not cheap, but are a stunning gift for the wine lover in your life.

A pair of these glasses from Green Man Wines or Searsons in Dublin will cost you €90.

Other brands

There are several value-driven options available in stores today. Some of the everyday glassware more than capable of delivering an enjoyable wine experience are:

- **Stolze Power Range** glasses, €38 for 4 from winelover.ie
- **Fox & Ivy** glasses, €14.99 for 4 from Tesco
- **Ikea Dyrgrip** Glasses, €10 for 4 from Ikea Ireland

Decanters

The next wine accessory that is essential to your repertoire is a good-quality decanter - bearing in mind, as I have mentioned previously, that you can use a jug or a large cup or anything really. The most important thing is that the wine is travelling quickly from the bottle and swallowing up plenty of air as it flows into the decanter.

Resting your wine is also important. This can be done easily in a good-quality decanter. There is a far wider circumference of the liquid that can access air than there would be if the wine was resting in the bottle. Air is conducive to freeing the flavours in the liquid into aromas that percolate in the decanter. After an hour or two, the difference in your wine will be marked – the flavours are more prominent and tannins are softened.

I'm sure you don't really want to serve your wine from a jug or a cup or any old kitchen item you found. Wine is a sensory experience and perception is key. Pouring from a beautiful decanter adds to the luxury and the pleasure of the wine.

The other reason you may want to use a decanter is to remove sediment from a wine, in particular with red wines that may have a little age on them. Because these wines have been produced in a heavier style, and the skins were heavily pressed to gain more colour and tannins, these sediments begin to form over time. The colour fades and the sediments increase. They're not harmful to consume, nonetheless they're unpleasant on the tongue.

To remove the sediments, hold the neck of the bottle of wine over a candle at a forty-five-degree angle. This way you can see the sediments gathering in the neck of the bottle. You continue to pour the wine gently into the decanter, allowing the liquid to pass over the trapped sediments. Twist the bottom of the bottle slowly as you pour, and this will ensure some of the sediments will stick to the bottle before they even reach the neck. This ensures a clean liquid in the decanter.

There are a number of places to acquire a nice decanter. Young, robust and tannic wines require a wider decanter to increase the airflow and capabilities of aeration. Older wines benefit far greater from a decanter with a narrower neck as this will contain more of those delicate, older and softer aromas.

- Galway Crystal have coloured decanters for €29.95 (older wine).
- Galway Crystal also have a traditional ship-style decanter for €49.90 (younger wine).
- Riedel have a range of decanters including the Performance range starting from €39.90 (older wine).
- Gabriel Glas Alpha have a top of the range offering for €199 (younger wine).

Accessories

Aerators

Your next best wine gadget will be an aerator. This little implement is very handy when you buy a wine that is meant for ageing, and you want to open the wine up fairly rapidly. As I mentioned before, many of the wines we are drinking are a little too young. In an ideal world, the winemaker wants you to drink the reds three to five years after they are bottled. However, because of the nature of the commercial world we live in, we don't have the time to wait for three years – most of us want to wait for three weeks. So, decanting and airing are a necessary evil to highlight the features of the wine.

If you are opening the bottle and are only going to have a single glass, then an aerator is the gadget for you. An aerator is a plastic funnel that you hold in one hand over the wine

Aerator

glass. With the other hand you pour the wine into the aerator. As the wine travels through, it flows through many little air pockets. This vigorous motion for the wine adds more air as it travels to the glass. I have tried this many times, and it genuinely works.

Wine aerators are available from winelover.ie for €24.99.

Openers

The next necessary gadget for your repertoire is a waiter's friend, a common type of wine opener. This might seem a little obvious to many, but gone are the days of the double-hinged opener that requires a knee hold if the cork is a little stiff in the neck of the bottle.

The waiter's friend is small, light and compact. It uses a lever effect on the arm of the wine opener to make it super easy to open even those dreaded plastic corks that seem to expand within the bottle. They're cheap as chips and one of the handiest items in your kitchen. Very often, your local independent wine

Waiter's friend

stores will hand them out complimentary. Ask in your local O'Briens or independent wine store. If not, you can order on Amazon for less than €5.

Electric wine openers are a bit of a fad right now. I have used them a little and I can see the logic. When they are charged, you pop them on the top of the bottle and simply press the button. This will easily remove the cork, and then you press again to remove the cork from the screw within the wine opener. Very handy for those with any difficulties using their hands or with mobility in general.

They are available from an Irish site called The Wine Opener (thewineopener.com) for €37.

Electric wine opener

Stoppers

If you like sparkling wines and you don't buy them because you feel they won't stay fresh – you don't see the point of opening a bottle for just one glass when the wine will be flat a day later – a stopper is the answer.

Champagne stoppers are ideal. When you have finished pouring your wine and you're putting it back into the fridge, you pop the stopper into the top of the bottle.

There is a rubber seal that rests inside the bottle and the clasps come down over the lip of the bottle to tighten the rubber seal even more. This keeps bubbles in the wine twice as long.

Stopper

My top tip would be to pop the stopper on straight after pouring your glass of wine and put the bottle back into the fridge. This way you're keeping in as much carbon dioxide as you can. The longer you leave the bottle on the table in the heat and the light and the air, the more the bubbles disappear. Using the stopper in the correct way will ensure your bubbles stay fresh well into three or four days after opening.

These are available on Amazon for €7.

Wine pump

Another way to keep your wine fresh are wine pumps. This is a very simple method where you place the rubber stopper in the top of the bottle and use the plastic pump to extract all the air out of the bottle. When the air is removed, the rubber seal will feel firm and restricted. This means the oxygen has been removed and no more air will get in. Using this pump will keep your wine fresh for over a week if you are diligent with pumping after each pour.

These are available on the Irish site winelover.ie for €24.99.

Wine coolers

When we are dining at home, the last thing we need slowing us down is continuously taking the wine in and out of the fridge for repours. We need handy access and speed. Not many of us have those large wine buckets that look like the Sam Maguire Cup – most of us mere mortals are subjected to filling up an old bowl with water and ice to keep our whites chilled. And that's cool.

However, for ease of service and aesthetic, there are simple stainless-steel coolers that can live happily on the end of the dinner table. They're sleek in shape and they circulate the chilled air coming from the bottle, keeping the wine cool that bit longer.

For a Champagne that needs to be really chilled there are cooler packs that you can freeze, take out and then wrap around the bottle. These are the real deal in terms of keeping the wine at a particularly cold temperature, despite being in a warm room. Both are available from winelover.ie.

- Stainless-steel cooler for €29.99
- Vacu Vin Active Cooler Champagne Platinum €24.99

Wine cooler

Coravin

A coravin is a really impressive tool if you're into your fancy wine gadgets. It allows you to pour wine from a bottle by way of a needle without having to remove the cork. You see this used

Coravin

often in high-end restaurants that sell wine by the glass. You can buy one in good independent wine stores or Brown Thomas.

Wine subscriptions

A wine subscription is always a fantastic gift for any wine lover you know – and, better yet, for yourself. They're a wonderful idea. Usually they are monthly and it's a great way to taste wines that you may not necessarily buy otherwise. The subscription consists of new and off-the-beaten-track wines with wine notes, food pairings and producer notes. There are a few companies in Ireland who do them.

- Wines Direct are based in Mullingar and have a monthly subscription called 'Explorers Wine Subscription'. There are four monthly plans – starting at €60 for three bottles, tasting notes and 5 per cent discount on all other wines, up to €150 a month for six months with extras such as tasting notes, a notebook, complimentary bubbles on your anniversary and 15 per cent discount on all wines.
- Wine Spark is a Dublin-based wine company that offers a completely different subscription. This model works on paying a yearly subscription of €120 and this gives you access to all the wines in the catalogue at cost price. So, a bottle of wine that normally retails for €30 you can buy for €19.98. A wine that normally retails for €23 you can buy for €16.53. This yearly sign-up also includes free

delivery on your wines and access to producer notes and an average discount of over 40 per cent on all wines.

- Boxofwine.ie are an online wine company offering subscriptions that are based events likes birthdays, Mother's Day, Christmas, etc. These boxes of wine are €49 and you can opt out at any time. A quiz is taken to determine your preferences and the next set of wines are based on your answers.

Another thoughtful wine gift for the one you love is a monthly subscription to *Decanter* magazine, which is a cornucopia of what's happening in the wine world today. I absolutely love this magazine. There's plenty in terms of wine ratings, articles, fascinating facts and a peek into the global producers. For a wine lover, it's a great monthly read to keep up to speed with wine reviews, wine investments and general scandal and gossip from the wine world. Its €109 per year – that's less than €9 a month, so well worth it.

Wine-cab-u-laree

An Expert's Glossary

Studying wine is a long and never-ending process. There are many courses you can take and hundreds and thousands of wines that you must taste to pass your exams. I know, it sounds dreadful, doesn't it?

During my training, I distinctly remember our wine lecturer, a softly spoken English lady, describing the white wines as 'crushed rocks' – 'bruised peaches' I am just about able for, but crushed rocks! I've yet to meet a person that will salivate at the thought of crushed rocks. They say bullshit baffles brains, so I decided to do my own research on all these ridiculously vague terms.

To be honest, I often question my place in an industry that thrives on nondescript, empty words. I am definitely a pragmatist by nature, and this wishy-washy mumbling is a step too far. Yes, I understand that there's an air of mystery and intrigue that must be created around a bottle of wine that might cost

€100. But words like 'zippy', 'structured', 'round', 'supple' and 'grippy' are of no use to an everyday wine drinker like me.

Sometimes, wine is so ridiculously described that I often wonder has the author giggled a little at the complete and utter bafflement they may be causing to the reader. Secretly, they may be choosing these scatterbrained words to really mess with our heads, to make it as difficult and elitist as possible to just choose a decent Malbec or a good-quality Rioja. The wine world loves an aul' ambiguous tone to a wine descriptor.

With that in mind, I have created my own glossary of wine words that will help you to make sense of the world of wine.

A

ABV Alcohol by volume: the alcohol levels described in percentage on a wine label. The average bottle of wine has between 9 per cent and 16 per cent alcohol.

acidity Fresh sensation experienced after tasting a wine. Acids in the wine make your saliva glands water (think fizzy jellies or a slice of lemon), and this excess saliva cleans your tongue after each sip. Genius for cleansing your palate after a bite of rich foods.

aeration Giving air to wine – 'letting it breathe'. This means enabling oxygen to come in contact with the wine, which can literally open your wine to even more flavours. A short time of oxygen exposure will also soften the tannins in your wine, giving it a smoother feel when it is in your mouth. Decanters are great for aeration.

aftertaste (finish) The taste of the wine that lingers in your mouth after it has been swallowed. This is a great way to judge the quality of wine. The longer the aftertaste, the better the wine. When tasting, do a time check and see how long the aftertaste lasts. You'll be surprised to see how many big factory-made wines have literally no after-taste.

ageing Process of storing wine in barrels, tanks or bottles in controlled conditions for a longer duration so the wine can develop complexity and extra flavours.

aggressive Usually refers to the acidity – if the acidity is too high then the wine is too tart. It can also refer to tannins that are too gripping on your gums.

alcohol (ethanol) Chemical produced from the fermentation process. It differentiates a wine from simple grape juice. Alcohol is felt by the warmth at the back of your throat. You should never feel too harsh a burn – if you do, the wine is out of balance.

alcoholic fermentation (primary fermentation) This is the process by which the yeasts on the grape skins react with the grape sugars and produce alcohol, carbon dioxide and heat. The final product is wine.

angular A wine that has a light and lean feeling in your mouth. It is the opposite of a full, rich-bodied wine.

anthocyanins Pigments found in red grapes that give the wine its colour. These are also full of antioxidants, making red wine a slightly more beneficial wine to consume.

appassimento Italian term for drying harvested grapes, which is traditionally done on straw mats. This can last from a few weeks up to several months to raisin the grapes and concentrate the sugars and flavours. This process is used in making Amarone and Recioto and is now commonly used in Puglia and Sicily.

appellation (Appellation Origine Protégée) Name given to a defined wine region found in France. These regions are strictly controlled and measured. The appellation name on the label means the wine has passed quality levels. Names like Sancerre, Pouilly-Fuissé and Vacqueyras are all appellations.

aroma Smell of the wine. There's huge importance to the various smells of wine, as they can signify if the wine is good, bad, off, old or just plain boring. Because of this, us wine nerds spend a lot of time smelling the wine, which is also crucial for enhancing the taste of the wine.

attack Usually refencing the strong initial impression you get from a wine, i.e. if the wine jumps out of the glass with pungent, vibrant aromas. For example, you can almost smell a Marlborough Sauvignon Blanc from New Zealand from the other side of the room.

astringent When the wine creates a drying, unpleasant feeling in your mouth from tannins that are too powerful. A simple way to overcome this is to swirl the wine vigorously in the glass or decant the full bottle to soften those harsh tannins. Snacking on a bite of food - such as a piece of cheese or cured meats - will melt away the tannins.

austere Wine that is subtle in taste. This is often used to describe a very young wine that is muted in flavour and seems to be lacking.

B

Bacchus Roman god of winemaking.

balance All the parts that make up the wine – the acids, alcohol, sugars and tannins – and whether or not these are all in balance with each other. This is a crucial part of understanding wine. Think about an orange. Some days, you get a really tart, sour orange that's almost inedible. Other days, you get a particularly sweet orange, that's just too sickly. And then on a random day, you get an orange that just hits the spot. Its sweet, fresh and delicious, and this is when you pay little attention to the parts of the orange because they all just fit together. You're enjoying the harmonious flavours of the orange so much that you forget to analyse it. It's all delicious. The same can be said for a well-balanced wine. All the parts are seamlessly working together so the wine is neither too tart nor too sweet.

Balthazar 12-litre bottle.

barrel/barrique Vessel in which a wine can be aged. They're made from oak and are generally from the US or France. It is the producer's choice to age the wine in a new or old oak barrel, depending on the level of oak flavour they want in their wine.

barrel fermented When a wine has been fermented in an oak barrel. The main difference is that the wine will have a softer, rounder feel when it's oak fermented. There may even be subtle flavours of butter, candyfloss or vanilla that come from this process. The majority of wines on the shop shelves are fermented in stainless-steel tanks, as they're larger and cheaper to use.

bâtonnage French term used for stirring the lees – the dead yeast cells in the liquid. By stirring them, you can add more weight, flavour and texture to the wine. This is a very popular winemaking technique used in white-wine production.

beefy Full-bodied, mouth-filling wine with big tannins, and rich in alcohol and flavours.

biodynamic Style of farming/vineyard-management technique based on the writings of Austrian philanthropist Rudolph Steiner that is now being adopted into the wine world. It involves using lunar cycles to dictate the planting, sowing, pruning and harvesting times. This style of farming uses absolutely no chemicals and is certified by a governing body called Demeter. It will clearly state this cert on the bottle if it is approved. Most of the top wineries in Burgundy are changing to this method. It's expensive but worth it.

bitter Taste sensation that is sensed on the back of the tongue and caused by powerful tannins.

Blanc de Blancs Champagne made only from white grapes – mainly Chardonnay grapes.

Blanc de Noirs Champagne made only from red grapes – Pinot Noir or Pinot Meunier.

blend When one or more grapes are fermented and then blended together to create a style of wine. Each grape gives a unique flavour or characteristic to the wine to add depth.

blush (rosé wine) Wine made from red grapes, but where the grape skin is removed during fermentation, so the wine is pink.

bodega Spanish term for a winery.

body Refers to the weight of the wine and how it feels in your mouth. A light-bodied wine should have the weight of water in your mouth; a full-bodied wine should have the weight of a full-fat milk. The weight of a wine is an easy way to understand what your preferences are and, further still, what you are in the mood for.

Bordeaux Area in south-west France that is considered one of the most significant and expensive wine-producing regions in the world.

Botrytis cinerea Desirable mould, known as 'noble rot', that breaks the skins of the grapes and causes dehydration, like a shrivelled raisin. This leads to the sugars in the grapes being concentrated and results in sweeter wines. This condition happens when vines are located close to lakes or rivers, though only in exceptional years. Therefore, the supply is extremely limited and the prices can be high. Used for sweet-wine production.

bouquet Aromas in an aged wine.

brett A set of yeasts that are found in the winery that can spoil wine. Usually red wine is more at risk. You can recognise the spoilage by barnyard or mousey aromas.

bright Acidity in lighter red wines.

brilliant A tasting note for wines that appear sparkling clear.

brooding Deep, dark red that is from rich, ripe, dark alcohol-laden berries.

Brut French term for a dry Champagne.

buttery Taste note for Chardonnay. A butter or buttered-toast character is found in richer styles of Chardonnay that are aged in barrels. Cheap oaking can lead to over-buttery tones. These wine are commercially very unpopular.

C

canopy Encompasses the shoots and leaves of the vine that can cover and shade the grapes in either extreme heat or excessive rainfall.

cantina Italian word for a winery.

carbon dioxide This gas is a by-product of fermentation. This is also how sparkling wines are made, by bottling the wine early and trapping all the natural carbon dioxide within the bottle.

carbonic maceration A process that helps make softer, more fruit-forward wines. Entire bunches of grapes are placed in vats and filled with carbonic gas when winemakers want to soften the tannins and create a juicy-style red that's easy to drink. It is viewed as a super-fast way to produce cheap everyday red wines.

casa Spanish word for house, as opposed to a winery.

Cava Spanish term used for the country's sparkling wines that are made by the traditional method. Literally means 'cave' or 'cellar'.

cedar Often used to describe a scent found in Bordeaux wines, especially from the Médoc appellations. These can smell of cedar wood or even a small cigar box.

cépage French word for grape variety.

Champagne Sparkling wine made in the region north-east of Paris called Champagne.

château French word for castle but, in everyday terms, means the 'estate' in which a wine is made.

claret Old-fashioned term used mostly in Great Britain that refers to Bordeaux wine. Originally, wines were very pale in colour and claret was the adaption of the French word *clairet* for clear.

clean Fresh on the palate and free of any faults.

closed Young wines whose flavours are not showing well. A good swirl or a decant will help closed wines.

cloying Wines that are too sweet and lack acidity, therefore they feel like they're sticking to the inside of your mouth.

CNP (Châteauneuf-du-Pape) One of the most famous wine regions in the world, located in Avignon, France. It was governed by the Pope and the Catholic Church for over 80 years. It is a very popular wine in the Irish market.

coarse Wine that is considered rough in texture and harsh to sip. This might be a super-dry red with big tannins.

colheita Portuguese term for a vintage Port.

concentrated Wines that show plenty of fruit, richness and depth of flavour, as well as being rich and full-bodied on the palate. The opposite of light wine.

commune French term for small village that is usually a part of an appellation – such as Petit Chablis, Fleurie, Pouilly-Fumé.

complex Wine that has many layers of flavours and aromas. Layers of flavours will come from natural grape flavours but also from the fermentation, oak ageing or, indeed, bottle ageing. A combination of richness, depth and flavour intensity.

cooper Barrel maker.

cooperage Place where they specialise in making barrels.

cooperative Wine organisation within a town that is owned and managed by a group of vineyard owners who bottle their wine under one label and share the profits. Often wines are produced from grapes grown by several members of the cooperative. Wine cooperatives are typically associated with cheaper, often bulk, wine, but are truly the lifeblood of everyday drinking French, Spanish and Italian wines.

coravin Implement used to pour wine out of a bottle through a needle without removing the cork. This tool is extremely useful for high-end restaurants that wish to sell wine by the glass.

cork Wooden bark that is specially shaped and cut to fit the neck of a bottle for sealing the bottle closed.

corkage fee Fee charged by restaurants when guests bring their own bottle of wine rather than ordering from the wine list. In Ireland, it can vary anywhere from €10 to €20 per bottle.

corked Wine that smells mouldy and of wet wool. This is a result of the cork being under attack from a naturally airborne fungus. It is extremely difficult to prevent but happens in fewer than 6 per cent of wines globally. The correct term for the fungal attack is 'trichloroanisole', or TCA.

crianza Spanish qualification for wine which must have been aged for at least two years. Reds must spend at least one year in oak; whites must spend at least six months.

crisp Usually refers to a white wine that is filled with pleasant acidity and a light body.

Crémant Sparkling wine in France from outside of the Champagne region. The interesting thing about Crémant is that it is aged for one year, as opposed to two years for Champagne, but has just as much quality and flavour as an entry-level Champagne. Probably the best value-for-money wines in France. Each region is permitted to use their own grape varieties, therefore you get a whole host of new flavours from Crémant.

Cru French term that generally refers to a vineyard or group of vineyards that have similar characteristics and, as a result, are classified together. In Bordeaux, the highest-quality wines are called Premiers Cru and in Burgundy, Grands Cru.

cuvée Special blend, barrel or bottling of a specific wine.

D

decadent Rich, opulent wines with mouth-filling textures – decadence in a wine is a positive thing.

decanting Practice of slowly and carefully pouring wine from a bottle into a larger container to remove sediment from wine before drinking, the sediment remains in the original bottle. This is also beneficial for giving the wine air. You don't need a fancy decanter – you can use a jug or a large cup. What's important is the motion of the wine coming out of the bottle, picking up air as it is poured.

delicate Light-body to medium-body wines with generous flavours. A desirable quality in wines such as Pinot Noir, Riesling, Chenin Blanc and Sauvignon Blanc.

Demeter The non-profit organisation that promotes and certifies biodynamic farming. The symbol will generally be found on the back label of the wine bottle.

demi-sec (half-dry) A wine is classified as dry when it has less than 7 grams of sugar per litre. A demi-sec will have 32 to 50 grams per litre of residual sugar. It is quite often associated with Champagne, where the scale from driest to sweetest is:

- *Brut nature* less than 3 grams of sugar per litre
- *extra Brut* less than 6 grams of sugar per litre
- *Brut* up to 12 grams of sugar per litre
- *extra-dry (extra-sec)* 12 to 17 grams of sugar per litre
- *dry (sec)* 17 to 32 grams of sugar per litre

- *demi-sec* 32 to 50 grams of sugar per litre
- *doux* 50 grams or more per litre

depth Wine with extra layers of flavour and concentration, making the wine feel deep, rich and serious – a clear sign of excellence. One of the best ways to understand quality wine is to understand the concentration of flavours. This comes from high-quality fruit in the vineyard, and it literally means the wine is especially flavoured from these top-quality berries.

developing Wine that is starting to show signs of age in terms of its flavour, aroma or colour. Flavours change from unripe to overripe fruit. For example, a youthful wine will have aromas of green apples and lemons, and this will develop into overripe toffee apples and baked lemons with a hint of caramel. Basically, flavours and aromas sweeten as they age.

Dionysis Greek god of wine.

DO (Denominación de Origen) One of Spain's regulatory classification systems, used to determine the grape varieties, alcohol levels and yields of a wine region. In 1991, a higher regulatory level, Denominación de Origen Calificada (DOCa), was established.

domaine French word for 'estate' or 'winery'. Commonly used in Burgundy. Bordeaux concentrates more on *château*.

dry Taste sensation often as a result of big tannins that cause a puckering sensation in the mouth – the opposite of sweet. If you like a dry red wine, more often than not you enjoy tannins, the components that will dry your mouth.

E

early picking Undertaken when the producer wants a wine with low alcohol. Because the grape sugars directly correlate to the amount of alcohol, if you pick early, you have lower grape sugars, therefore lower alcohol in your finished wine.

earthy Soil-like flavour in wine. Strange as it may seem, earthiness is a desired characteristic when talking about the flavours in wine. In small amounts, the aromas or flavours can add complexity. However, it is a subtle balance between too little earthiness and too much. Pinot Noir from Burgundy is often considered to have a wild mushroom or cabbage flavour to it. I know, crazy, eh, wishing your wine smelled of cabbage!

elegant Balanced, harmonious well-made wine; it is subtle rather than a highly extracted, rich wine. A common nondescript adjective.

elevage Wine spending time in a bottle while it settles and ages. The length of time varies greatly. It can range from a couple of weeks to a number of years depending on the producer and the quality required.

enology The science of wine and winemaking.

en primeur The first offering of a wine from an estate of very high value. It is mostly used in Bordeaux and it is in reference to the early market prices at which investors will buy wine to store for many years, either to drink or sell on.

estate Property of land, which will include vineyards and possibly a winery to make the wine. You will see on the back label if the wine is 'estate bottled'.

ethanol *See* alcohol.

extracted The drawing of flavours, tannins and colour from grapes. A light extraction will be a gentle pressing for an hour or so. A deep extraction will be a longer time on the skins after crushing and a far firmer squeeze on the grapes, which means more tannins, more colour, more body and more flavour. The extraction is also achieved through maceration (soaking the skins of the crushed grapes in the wine after fermentation), during which alcohol helps dissolve flavour, aroma and especially tannins – the same as soaking a teabag in hot water.

F

fat Full-bodied, high-alcohol wines that are low in acidity give a 'fat' or 'round' sensation on the palate.

fault Wine that has an undesirable character to it because of a fault in the winemaking or the cellaring of the wine. Some examples might be harsh tannins from a heavy extraction or brett (earthy, sour flavours) from an airborne fungus or cork taint.

feminine Wines with qualities such as smoothness, gentleness, finesse, elegance and delicacy. The term is slightly on the decline.

fermentation Process of turning sugars into alcohol, also known as alcoholic fermentation.

filtering Process of clarifying wine before bottling by removing solid particles. Wine is pumped through a screen or pad to remove the larger leftover grape and fermentation particles. Most wines are filtered to create a crystal-clear liquid and to remove potentially spoiling characters. Many natural wine-makers leave their wine unfiltered, giving it a hazy appearance.

fine lees Dead yeast cells that are killed off during the fermentation process. After fermentation, some wines are aged on their fine lees. Fine lees are used to add more richness, complexity and aromatics to a wine. This is also known as 'ageing sur lie' – Muscadet Sur Lie has been aged for three months plus on the dead yeast cells.

fining A step to clarify the wine after filtering. The producer will use agents, such as bentonite (powdered clay), isinglass (fish bladder), casein (milk protein), gelatine or egg whites, that combine with sediment particles and cause them to settle to the bottom, where they can be easily removed. When the fining material used is pure clay or from a non-animal source, the wine can be classified as vegan.

finish (aftertaste) Length of time you can taste the wine in your mouth after you've swallowed it. The finish is one of the clearest and easiest ways for you to judge the quality of the wine. The longer and more complex the finish, the better the wine.

flabby Wine that has very low acidity, so it doesn't make your mouth water. The wine leaves a sweetish residue that gives the feeling of a flabby wine.

fleshy Wine that gives rise to mouth-watering sensations. This is a medium-bodied wine that is mouth-filling, soft and generous.

flight When more than one wine is poured at the same time. In high-end restaurants, you may be given a flight of Bordeaux wines to taste. This is such a great way to compare and contrast flavours and weights. A great way to learn.

floral Aromas and flavours in certain grape varieties that have a floral tone to them. One famous example is the dark-violet flowers that are found in Syrah from the Rhône Valley.

flying winemaker A winemaker who travels and shares winemaking skills from one region of the world to another.

fortified wine Dessert wine or digestif. Standard wines that have alcohol distillate (spirit) added to them to boost their alcohol levels to 16–20 per cent ABV.

forward Wine that is open, full of flavour and ready to drink.

foxy Wine-tasting term similar to mould.

fruity Wine that smells of and has a flavour similar to fresh fruit.

G

Gran Reserva Spanish term used for wines that are aged in wood and bottles for at least five years before release.

Grand Cru (great growth) French term describing the best vineyards.

green Vegetal and underripe flavours in wine – not a good characteristic.

grip Firmness of texture that usually comes from tannins. Wine with grip is hard to drink and better to sip. Remember to swirl well in your glass and the tannins will melt away.

H

hard Wine that has too many tannins and becomes unpleasant.

harvest Picking grapes from the vineyard. Harvest time varies all over the world. It all depends on the success of the vintage and if the weather has aided quality vine production.

herbaceous Aroma or flavour similar to green – often an indication of underripe grapes or fruit grown in a cool climate like northern France or England. Flavours of fresh herbs – basil, oregano, rosemary and sage.

I

ice wine Wine made from frozen grapes, found in very cool climates.

Imperial 6-litre bottle.

J

Jeroboam Oversized bottle, equal to six regular 750 ml bottles.

L

late harvest Berries that are left to hang on the vine for longer than normal, so the sugars rise. Sweet wines are made from late-harvest berries.

lean Wines made in an austere style. Not necessarily a critical term, but when used as a term of criticism, it indicates a wine is lacking in fruit.

leather Aroma of old leather, most frequently associated with older red wines that have developed flavours. Leather aromas are often found in reds that were aged in old oak.

lees Dead yeast cells that remain after the fermentation has finished – often used to age the wine and therefore add body, flavour and texture.

legs Drops of wine that creep down the side of the wine glass. A higher alcohol wine will have visually thicker legs.

length (finish) Amount of time that taste, flavour or mouthfeel persist after swallowing a wine. The longer the length, the better the wine quality. Common descriptors are short, long and lingering.

lively Wines that are fresh, fruity and bright.

M

maceration Contact of grape skins with the flesh of the grapes during fermentation, extracting tannins, anthocyanins and aromas. Leaving the grape juice together with skins, stalks and seeds, which affects the extraction of the colour, tannins and flavour.

Magnum 1.5-litre bottle.

Malbec Hearty red grape of French origin now popular in Argentina.

maturation Process of ageing wine that improves its quality.

mature Ready to drink. The wine will not gain any additional complexity with longer bottle ageing. Also describes grapes when they are fully ripe.

minerality The aromas or tastes associated with experiencing flavours like stone or chalk

Mis en bouteille French term meaning 'put in bottle'. Noted on the back of a wine label, also with the name of the estate where the wine was bottled.

mousse Frothy head that forms at the surface of sparkling wine.

mouthfeel How a wine feels in your mouth. Many descriptors are related to texture - silky, smooth, velvety and rough. It is influenced by acidity (can be sharp), alcohol (can be hot), tannins (can be harsh) and sugar (can be thick or cloying).

N

Nebuchadnezzar Large bottle holding 15 litres, the equivalent of twenty regular wine bottles.

new oak The first time a barrel is used. With further uses, the wood imparts fewer flavours and tannins. Flavours associated with new oak include vanilla, cedar, toast and smoke.

New World wine Wines produced outside of the traditional wine-growing areas of Europe and North Africa. Includes Argentina, Australia, Chile, New Zealand, South Africa and the USA.

noble rot *See* Botrytis cinerea

non-vintage (NV) Wine blended with grapes grown in more than one vintage. This enables the producer to keep a house style from year to year. Many Champagnes and sparkling wines are non-vintage. Sherries and ruby ports are all non-vintage.

nose Aroma, the smell of the wine in the glass.

O

oaky Woody aromas and flavours in the wine that develop during maturation in oak barrels or by adding oak chips.

off-dry Wine that is slightly sweet.

old vine Wines made from very old vines – at least thirty years old.

open Wine that is ready to drink.

organic Grapes grown with lower volumes of chemical-based fertilisers, pesticides or herbicides. The qualifications for organic vary massively from country to country, so it's a fairly vague term. Remember natural or biodynamic wines are those completely without chemicals.

oxidation Wine that has been overexposed to air and has undergone a chemical change. All the fruit flavours have been killed off and only the acids and mouldy aromas are left.

P

palate Flavour or taste of a wine, also refers to the different sections of taste in the mouth. As the wine travels through the mouth, it first meets the front palate, then the mid-palate and finally the back palate – all taste different flavours, such as sweet, sour and bitter.

peak Period when a wine tastes its best. This is very subjective, just to make our lives even more confusing.

perfume All wines have perfume. Wines that bottle age will develop secondary non-fruit aromas – such as leather, tobacco, dried toast and mushroom.

Phylloxera Pesky minute insect that attacks the roots of grape vines.

Pinot Black or white grape variety from which Pinot Noir and Pinot Grigio are made.

pip Grape seed.

plonk Slang for cheap or low-quality wines.

port Deliciously sweet fortified wine made in the Douro Valley in Portugal – examples include Vintage, Tawny, Late Bottled Vintage, Ruby, White and others.

Premier Cru (first growth) Extremely high-quality vineyard, but still lower quality than Grand Cru.

primary aromas Aromas in wine that come from the grapes themselves and are part of the grape variety.

punt Dent at the bottom of a glass bottle. This is often associated with high-quality wines, but it is there to strengthen the bottle and to give the illusion that the bottle contains more liquid than it actually does.

R

racking Process of wine being transferred from one barrel to another to remove large sediments.

racy Wines with high acidity.

ratings Numbers given to wines to show how a taster ranks them against other wines. The most famous example is the 1–100 rating from Robert Parker – 90+ are considered good-quality wines; 95+ are considered excellent. A 100-point score will treble the value of your wine overnight.

reserve Overused term that signifies extra ageing time. It can have different meanings, depending on the producer and the country. Mostly, it refers to a producer's higher-quality wine. Spain and Italy are the only countries where this term is actually qualified and verified.

residual sugar (RS) The unfermented sugar that remains in a finished wine after the alcoholic fermentation. The amount of residual sugar left depends on the style of wine the winemaker is looking to produce. It is measured in grams per litre, and a dry wine is calculated to have anything less than 12 grams of residual sugar per litre.

rich Wine that displays ample texture, body and flavour, along with a long finish. All aspects of the wine are generous.

Right Bank Area in Bordeaux where wines from Pomerol, Saint-Émilion and other villages are located, to the east of the famous Garonne River.

Rioja Well-known region in northern Spain famous for oak ageing their red wines for many years before release. A super region for value-for-money wines.

rosé French word for 'pink'. Wines made from red grapes that have a far lighter colour.

round Wines that feel rich and succulent in your mouth. This trait can come from low-acid wines and wines produced from fruit when the tannins were allowed to ripen fully.

rustic Rough-textured, old-school wines that are often austere and lacking in vibrant fruit. It can also mean more of a simple country wine with character. The term can take on slightly different meanings, depending on the critic.

S

Sancerre Area in the Loire Valley famous for Sauvignon Blanc. This is the home of Sauvignon Blanc and a style of wine that is often emulated.

sec French term for 'dry'.

second wine Wine that is often produced from an estate's young vines, or from juice or grapes that are not considered to be at the required level of quality for the property's top wine. Very common to see these wines in Bordeaux.

secondary aromas Aromas of a mature wine. These wines develop non-fruit aromas like truffles, tobacco, leather, tar, cedar and spice. This is a wonderful thing and must be smelled to be believed.

secondary fermentation When wine is transferred into another vessel. This is a standard practice in Champagne production. The secondary fermentation takes place in the bottle.

sediment As a wine ages, tannins, pigments and other materials bond together. It will not harm you, but its bitter taste is not going to help your wine. You can remove sediment by decanting.

silky Wines that are low in tannins, so the wine feels polished in your mouth. Similar to velvety, but perhaps a little lighter.

smoky Aromas that generally stem from oak ageing. They can also come directly from smoke taint that has occurred in wildfires. Australia and California are developing techniques to try and minimise the smoke taints from wildfires.

sommelier Certified wine expert, who often works in a restaurant and specialises in selecting, purchasing, recommending and serving wine.

steely Tasting term describing acidic wines.

stony Aroma that comes from grapes that are grown in mineral-rich soils, generally limestone or slate, resulting in a steely, almost iron-like flavour and aroma. Very often associated with German Riesling, the grapes for which are grown on slate hills. Similar to minerality.

sulphites Natural compounds in wine that are a by-product of the fermentation process. They act as a preservative and keep wine fresh in the bottle for years. They do not give you head-aches, as the new-age wine bashers will tell you – there are more sulphites in a bag of crisps than a bottle of wine. A derivate of sulphur dioxide.

supple Tasting term for balanced wines with plenty of soft edges, i.e. not sharp in taste.

sur lie French term for a wine that is aged on its fine lees.

T

table wine Basic-level, everyday wine that is affordable.

tannins Natural compounds found in the skins, pips and stalks of grapes. They are used in winemaking for preserving wine and giving it structure. The tannins need to be ripe for the wine to feel smooth in your mouth.

tart Wines that are produced from unripe grapes. They are high in acidity and do not have enough pleasant fruit flavours.

tartaric acid Acid that helps to balance the wine, enhancing the colour, taste and mouthfeel. Winemakers may choose to add a little extra to help balance the wine. This can often present in the form of tartrate crystals that can gather on the end of the cork or appear in the bottom of your glass. They are totally harmless and safe to consume.

terroir French word that best describes local influences to grape growing, like the soils, the area's flora and fauna, and the local microclimate.

tertiary aromas The aromas that develop when the wine ages a little. They can consist of nuts, leather, spices and dried fruits.

tobacco Desired aroma often found in wines that have been oak aged.

Trocken German word for dry.

U

Umami Described as a flavour that spreads across your tongue. It refers to savoury miso, earthy, mushroom flavours. It is a Japanese word that literally translates to 'delicious savoury taste'. It is considered to be one of the primary tastes we have.

V

varietal Wine made from a single grape variety.

vegetal Undesirable aroma found in wines that have been made from unripe grapes.

vibrant Wines that are bright, fruit driven and exciting to taste.

vigneron/vigneronne French words for a winemaker.

vin French word for wine.

vinification Practice of winemaking.

vintage Year in which the grapes are harvested for the wine.

viticulture The study of vine growing.

vitis vinifera Latin term for the best-quality grape used specifically for winemaking.

volatile Wine smells of vinegar due to excess acetic acid, which develops when ethanol is exposed to oxygen.

W

weight How light or heavy the wine feels on your palate. The weight of the wine determines the style it is categorised in: does it have a light weight? Is it a rich full-bodied weight?

Y

yeast Element that reacts with the sugars to create alcohol (ethanol) in your wine. Yeasts can be natural and found on the skins of the grapes or can be bought in commercially. It is one of the most important aspects of winemaking.

yield Determines how much a vineyard produces each year. Yields are generally strictly controlled by local legislation to help quality control and diminish overproduction. Low yields will often produce better wines.

Always remember that these wine words are usually just describing either the texture of the wine or the flavours of the wine. Wine is a subject that people absolutely love to talk about and using these words will give you the ability to talk a little more about the nuances and delicacies in your wine.

What I try and do is think about the words pragmatically. For example, the term 'lean': literally just try and envisage the wine in a leaner form - thin, light and lean on flavours.

One of the most important things I could say about wine is that is it so subjective. At the end of the day, we all have different tastes, we all have different palates and we certainly all have different perspectives. What I might taste in a wine, you might struggle to taste and vice versa.

I guess this is all part of the mystique and fun with wine - no taste is ever the same between us all. Truthfully, you can bluff your way around, as long as you have the confidence and the know-how. But don't try too hard, as you'll do me out of a job.

Conclusion

We have come to the end of our wine journey together. I hope that this book has opened your mind and has armed you with the tools to choose your next wine with confidence.

I have put my heart and soul into this book for you. It is the culmination of twenty plus years working in the industry, spanning all aspects including wine buying, selling, serving and tasting. I absolutely have been where you might feel you are now: totally overwhelmed by the level of information you need just to buy a simple bottle of wine. It seems gargantuan. But just remember the first five points in the introduction are a great tool to use when you're staring into space in the aisles of your local wine shop. That is a good place to start.

Keep in mind that those who are trying to con you with flowery, vacuous words probably know less than you do: they're just better at bluffing. You don't need to go off and study for a wine diploma just to enjoy your favourite drink on a Saturday night – you just need to use this book as a reference guide whenever you feel lost.

Don't forget the most important thing: wine is there to be enjoyed so don't be intimidated by it. It is there to be shared and talked about, to be paired with delicious foods and snacks galore.

So, focus on your own tastes and what suits you. Like our good friend the New Yorker: drink your wine from a shoe, drink your wine watching Netflix, drink your wine too warm, too cold – just drink your wine and let it put a smile on your face.

Life is better with good-quality wine in it.

Acknowledgements

As I sit and write this, I am so incredibly grateful. It is an actual fizzing feeling. I have always loved writing, and thankfully never listened to my English secondary school teacher. Her hopes for me in a literary capacity were pretty low. But here I am just after writing a wine book. I certainly didn't see this one coming, but to say I am chuffed would be an understatement.

It is imperative for me to begin my thank you's with my children. Will, Jude and Beatrice, you will never understand the love and joy I have because you are in my life. We have been on a rollercoaster ride for the past couple of years, but I wouldn't want to do it with anyone else. I cherish everyday with you guys.

Thank you to my parents Joey and Ros. The past couple of years have not been easy, and you both have never faltered in your support for me and the kids.

Thank you to my sister Kate, who has always been there for

me. Through all that we have experienced over the years, we have laughed and cried in equal measures. Thank you for being there. Thank you also Matt, Oscar and Jules for entertaining and loving our family like no other.

To my brothers Manus and Joe, I love you both so much. We have had a colourful life filled with up's and down's but we always stick together. To Benny, Joey and Charlie, our Donegal brethren that light up our lives also.

I am a very lucky person to have so many close friends who listen to me and keep me going. Thank you Jen, Deb, James G, Amy, Paul, Nancy, James D, Mark H, Collette, Kevin, to name but a few.

A massive thanks to Ciara who reached out to me and brought this magical opportunity in to my world. I am forever grateful. Thank you also to Joanna and Stephen who have patiently guided this first timer through this process.

Thank you to my boss Laura, who has been nothing but patient and understanding throughout this process. I was offered my job and the book within hours of each other, so I feel very lucky that I had the opportunity to do both.

Thank you, Gideon, for minding our children while I worked away on this life-long dream.

Image sources

Motifs throughout: Nic & Lou

Page 53: Taste areas of the tongue – Peter Hermes Furian/ Shutterstock

Page 55: Flavour wheel – Cathal O'Gara

Page 72: Inside of a grape – baibaz/Shutterstock

Page 155: Champagne glass – cve iv/Shutterstock

Page 158: White wine glass – cve iv/Shutterstock

Page 160: Red wine glass – cve iv/Shutterstock

Page 162: Large red wine glass – cve iv/Shutterstock

Page 165: Dessert wine glass – cve iv/Shutterstock

Page 185: Crémant wine regions – Cathal O'Gara

Page 190: Prosecco region – Cathal O'Gara

Page 194: Wine bottle sizes – Cathal O'Gara

Page 198: Wine glasses through history – Cathal O'Gara

Page 200: Different wine glass sizes – cve iv/Shutterstock

Page 206: Aerator – Iurii Korolev/Shutterstock

Index

Index

Index